j 973.7349
R 361g

D1489274

2/2005   MAR 1 9 2005

HU

BATTLES
THAT CHANGED THE WORLD

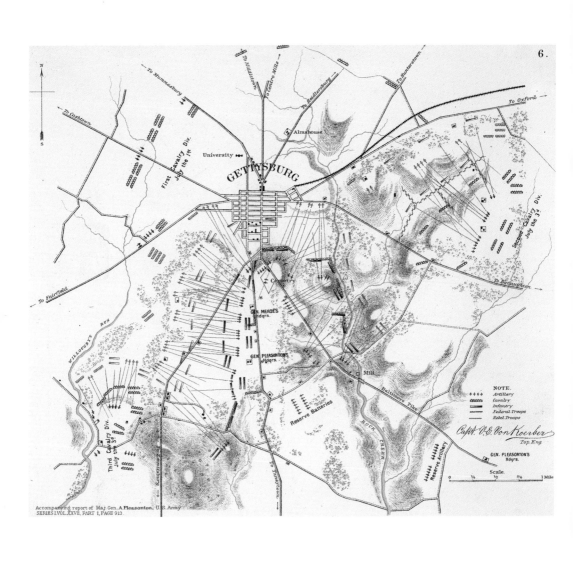

6.

N

S

To Mummasburg
To Middletown
To Centre Mills
To Shallersburg
To Oxford
To Cashtown
To Hunterstown

Almshouse

University

First Cavalry Div. July the 1st.

GETTYSBURG

Second Cavalry Div. July the 3d.

To Fairfield

Cemetery

GEN. MEADE'S Hdqrs.

GEN. PLEASONTON'S Hdqrs.

Mill

Baltimore Pike

ROCK CREEK

Reserve Batteries

WILLOUGHBY'S RUN

Third Cavalry Div. July the 3d.

Reserve Artillery

To Emmittsburg
To Taneytown

NOTE.
Artillery
Cavalry
Infantry
Federal Troops
Rebel Troops

Capt. V. C. Von Koerber
Top. Eng.

GEN. PLEASONTON'S Hdqrs.

Scale.
0   ¼   ½   ¾   1 Mile

Accompanying report of Maj. Gen. A. Pleasonton, U.S. Army.
SERIES I VOL. XXVII, PART 1, PAGE 913.

GETTYSBURG

EARLE RICE JR.

CHELSEA HOUSE PUBLISHERS
PHILADELPHIA

FRONTISPIECE: Map of Gettysburg showing the Civil war artillery, cavalry, and infantry positions.

CHELSEA HOUSE PUBLISHERS

EDITOR IN CHIEF Sally Cheney
DIRECTOR OF PRODUCTION Kim Shinners
CREATIVE MANAGER Takeshi Takahashi
MANUFACTURING MANAGER Diann Grasse

STAFF FOR GETTYSBURG

EDITOR Lee Marcott
PICTURE RESEARCHER Patricia Burns
PRODUCTION ASSISTANT Jaimie Winkler
COVER AND SERIES DESIGNER Keith Trego
LAYOUT 21st Century Publishing and Communications, Inc.

http://www.chelseahouse.com

First Printing

1 3 5 7 9 8 6 4 2

Library of Congress Cataloging-in-Publication Data

Rice, Earle.
    The Battle of Gettysburg / by Earl Rice Jr.
        p. cm. — (Battles that changed the world)
Summary: Explains the events leading up to the Battle of Gettysburg, the defining battle of
the Civil War, and describes the battle and its aftermath.
Includes bibliographical references and index.
    ISBN 0-7910-6684-3 (hardcover) — ISBN 0-7910-7108-1 (pbk.)
    1. Gettysburg (Pa.), Battle of, 1863—Juvenile literature. [1. Gettysburg (Pa.), Battle of,
1863. 2. United States—History—Civil War, 1861-1865—Campaigns.] I. Title. II. Series.
E475.53 .R48 2002
973.7'349—dc21

                                                                                        2002003631

CONTENTS

Brandy Station: Overture on Horseback

Ordered to advance against Confederate forces near Culpeper, Virginia in June 1863, Major General Alfred Pleasonton and his men confronted General Jeb Stuart and the Confederate cavalry at the Battle of Brandy Station. While both generals claimed a measure of victory, the battle made it clear to southern forces that their Yankee adversaries were far from inept.

I n early June of 1863, Major General Joseph "Fighting Joe" Hooker, commander of the Union Army of the Potomac, received word from federal signal officers that units of General Robert E. Lee's Confederate Army of Northern Virginia had been sighted on the march, moving westward from the lines around Fredericksburg, Virginia. Subsequent intelligence reports indicated that advance elements of Confederate infantry, artillery, and Major General James Ewell Brown "Jeb" Stuart's cavalry were halted at Culpeper Court House, approximately 30 miles up the Rappahannock River from Fredericksburg.

On June 7, Hooker, suspecting that Stuart was preparing for

General Pleasonton (1824-1897) was a graduate of West Point, as were many officers on both sides of the battle lines. His leadership and the courage of his men at the Battle of Brandy Station showed that the Confederate cavalry was not invincible after all.

a raid, summoned his own cavalry commander, the handsome, dark-eyed Major General Alfred Pleasonton. He ordered him to advance against Stuart's cavalry and engage them. Bolstering Pleasonton's three cavalry divisions with two infantry brigades—about 12,000 men—

Hooker directed him "to disperse and destroy the rebel force assembled in the vicinity of Culpeper, and to destroy his trains and supplies of all descriptions to the utmost of your ability."[1]

Hooker tapped a spot on his map labeled Brandy Station and continued. "If you can't cut him [Stuart] to pieces, at least shake him up—put him on the run, harass him—*anything* to stop Lee dead in his tracks," he said. "You have at least a 30-mile march. Take your entire corps and leave tomorrow."[2]

The word spread fast in Pleasonton's camp. Artillery Major Charles S. Wainwright noted in his diary: "Something is certainly in the wind . . . . The Cavalry, I hear, are to make a reconnoissance [*sic*] or demonstration towards Culpepper [*sic*]."[3]

Pleasonton's troopers prepared for action against their Confederate nemesis with a keen sense of purpose and grim determination. In slightly more than two years of war, the Union cavalry had, in general, proved to be no match for its Confederate counterparts. But times were changing. Yankee cavalrymen had matured into veteran warriors, skilled in the arts of horsemanship and killing. And they yearned to rid themselves of the stigma of inferiority that had demeaned them since the start of the war. They were *ready!*

Meanwhile, as Pleasonton's camp bustled with battle preparations, Jeb Stuart's horsemen were staging a grand review for their cavalier leader in the rolling countryside north of Culpeper around Brandy Station. Stuart, his florid face mostly covered by a reddish-brown mustache and spreading beard, looked on through penetrating blue eyes, his five-foot-ten, wide-shouldered frame sitting erect in the saddle. He loved few things more than the pageantry of mounted troops passing in review. And he exemplified in his personal attire the flamboyant image that he had worked hard to create. Of his propensity for sartorial elegance, Douglas Southall Freeman, one of Stuart's biographers, writes:

> The Army boasted nothing to excel [Stuart's] con-
> spicuous uniform—a short gray jacket covered with
> buttons and braid, a gray cavalry cape over his
> shoulder, a broad hat looped with a gold star and
> adorned with a plume, high jack boots and gold
> spurs, an ornate and tasseled yellow sash, gauntlets
> that climbed almost to his elbows. His weapons were
> a light French saber and a pistol, which he carried in
> a black holster. . . . When he gave commands, it was
> in a clear voice that could reach the farthest
> squadron of a regiment in line.[4]

But on this day, June 7, even Stuart's resonant commands likely fell short of reaching the most distant members of his newly enlarged command.

A gray line of soldiers stretched across the open spaces for more than a mile before him, while three bands filled the air with rousing military measures and 10,000 cavalry-men and their mounts passed jauntily in review. After their passing, the cavalry brigades staged a mock battle, charging the horse artillery with sabers flashing in the sunlight and wild shouts echoing over the thunder of galloping hooves. The artillerists met their charge with the roar of 22 batteries of cannon loaded with blank cartridges, adding to the clamor and realism of the great pretense. Men cheered; ladies applauded.

"Stirred or frightened by this gaudy climax," writes Shelby Foote, one of the preeminent chroniclers of the Civil War, "several ladies fainted, or pretended to faint, in the grandstand which Jeb had set up for them along one side of the field."[5]

Stuart repeated the grand review on June 8 for the late-arriving General Lee. At Lee's request, Stuart omitted the

General Jeb Stuart (1833-1864) was known for his saber-wielding cavalry. After the Battle of Brandy Station, the Confederate cavalry began a decline from which it would not recover.

mock battle, which Lee viewed as a waste of gunpowder and horseflesh. Even without the bombastic display, the colorful performance filled the equally colorful Stuart with pride. As Lee noted in a letter home, his cavalry chief "was in all his glory."[6] Beyond pageantry and pride, however, as a result of the second review, most of Stuart's 10,000 troopers remained concentrated overnight near Brandy Station.

That night, the plumed commander and his officers

attended a ball in their honor. Stuart appeared completely at ease to those in attendance. And why not? After all, to his way of thinking, he commanded the finest cavalry in the world and certainly had nothing to fear from his Yankees opposites. Like his fellow Confederate cavalrymen, he held the fighting ability of the blue-clad horsemen in great disdain. Jeb was about to find cause for reevaluating his federal foes.

While Stuart and his officers danced the night away, General Pleasonton and six brigades of Union cavalry—a mounted force about equal in strength to Stuart's—and one of infantry proceeded upriver from Falmouth to their preattack destinations. Pleasonton, who planned on launching a two-pronged thrust at the enemy, split his forces into two main elements. He ordered the first element, under Brigadier General John Buford, to cross the Rappahannock at Beverly Ford, northwest of Brandy Station. And he directed the second element, led by Brigadier General David McM. Gregg, four miles downstream to Kelly's Ford, southeast of the enemy stronghold. Pleasonton hoped to surprise Stuart in a classic pincer movement and crush the life out of him.

Pleasonton set up headquarters for the night in the home of William Bowen Sr., located about a mile from Beverly Ford. A young cavalry captain whose fighting prowess had caught the general's attention wrote a letter to his fiancée from the Bowen house that night: "I never was in better spirits than I am at this moment [but if] something happens to me . . . I want all my letters burned."[7] His words expressed the conflicting emotions he apparently felt on the eve of battle—a supreme confidence tempered by a keen awareness of the imminence of death.

At dawn on the morning of June 9, 1863, a dense fog shrouded the Rappahannock basin in an eerie light, as Buford's division of Union cavalry splashed across the shallow waters of Beverly Ford. Pleasonton accompanied

General John Buford (seated in this photograph) commanded an element of the Union cavalry at Brandy Station. Southern forces had underestimated the tenacity of the Union horsemen, who by 1863 had become seasoned warriors.

them on the right wing, along with the young captain who had won his favor, a good man to have along in a fight. One of the young captain's peers had described him earlier as "a slim young man with almost flaxen hair, looking more like a big boy . . . with the cheek of a government mule."[8] None would deny that the young captain was as brash as they come. But boldness becomes a warrior.

Colonel Benjamin F. "Grimes" Davis's brigade of Buford's division led the way, with the Eighth New York Cavalry in front. Davis rode in front of his former regiment. In no time, rebel pickets (sentries) opened fire on the advancing Yankees. Davis immediately ordered a charge. "When Colonel Davis found the rebels he did not stop at anything, but went for them heavy," a New York trooper asserted. "I believe he liked to fight the rebels as well as he liked to eat."[9]

Davis, a Mississippian who had remained loyal to the Union, waved his troopers forward with drawn saber and plunged straight at the Confederate battery. Suddenly, the Sixth Virginia Cavalry, of Brigadier General William E. "Grumble" Jones's brigade, struck Davis's troopers, stopped them short of the rebel horse artillery units, and sent them reeling backward. Lieutenant R. O. Allen of the Sixth Virginia engaged Davis in a pistol duel, snapping off three shots at the Union colonel. Allen's third shot struck him in the forehead, toppling the colonel from his steed. He was dead before hitting the ground.

The Confederate cannoneers now turned a pair of guns into position and started firing down the Beverly's Ford Road at Buford's troops. Their action enabled the rest of the rebel horse artillery to withdraw and to set up new positions at the Mary Emily Gee house and at the St. James Church—structures located atop knolls on opposite sides of the road. A surprised Jeb Stuart heard the sounds of gunfire from his headquarters at the top of Fleetwood Hill, overlooking Brandy Station. He realized that the sounds of battle meant that Union forces had crossed the river and immediately sent scattered brigades to confront the attack. The new artillery positions established a foundation upon which to form a Confederate line. Most of Jones's command formed a line to the left of their artillery, while Brigadier General Wade Hampton's brigade took up positions to the right.

Buford attempted to break through the rebel line and a savage battle ensued, with the Sixth Pennsylvania Cavalry bearing the brunt of the carnage. At the outset of the fighting, regimental commander Major Robert Morris Jr. was captured when his horse fell attempting to leap a ditch. Major Henry C. Whelan took command and later recalled their charge across 800 yards of open field under heavy Confederate fire: "We dashed at them, squadron front with drawn sabres, and as we flew along—our men yelling like demons—grape and canister [shot] were poured into our left flank and a storm of rifle bullets on our front." The Pennsylvanians drove the rebels into and through the woods, matching their sabers against the enemy's pistol fire. "Our brave fellows cut them out of the saddle and fought like tigers," Whelan continued, "until I discovered they were on both flanks, pouring a cross fire of carbines and pistols on us, and then tried to rally my men and make them return the fire with their carbines."[10]

The view of men and horses clashing in deathly struggle was no less intense from the other side. Long after the battle, gunner George M. Neese, of Captain Roger P. Chew's battery of Confederate horse artillery, recalled that "hundreds of glittering sabres instantly leaped from their scabbards, gleamed and flashed in the morning sun, then clashed with a metallic ring, searching for human blood, while hundreds of little puffs of white smoke gracefully rose through the balmy June air from discharging firearms all over the field in front of our batteries . . . the artillerymen stood in silent awe gazing on the struggling mass in our immediate front.[11]

After his first attack on the Confederate line failed, Buford conceded that he could not dislodge their artillery and decided to anchor his right flank on the Hazel River and try to turn the enemy's left. But to his left, on a piece of high ground called Yew's Ridge, and along a stone wall to its front, Brigadier General W. H. F. "Rooney" Lee's brigade blocked his advance. At the cost of heavy losses, Buford's federals finally seized control of the stone wall. Then, to the amazement of Buford and his men, the Confederates began to pull back. Buford learned later that they had backed off to meet a new threat—Stuart's second surprise of the day. Another enemy force at least as strong as Buford's had eluded the pickets at Kelly's Ford and was bearing down on Brandy Station, two miles to Stuart's rear.

Stuart improvised quickly to grapple with Gregg's newly arrived Union division.

"The result," writes Shelby Foote, "as he regrouped his forces arriving from north and south to meet the double threat, was hard fighting in the classic sense, headlong charges met by headlong countercharges, with sabers, pistols, and carbines employed hand to hand to empty a lot of saddles."[12] In this frenzied action, Stuart lost Fleetwood Hill, regained it, lost it again, and regained it again, as the hill changed hands any number of times during the afternoon.

At the height of the action, the flaxen-haired captain whose fighting prowess had caught the eye of General Pleasonton led elements of Buford's First Cavalry Brigade in a hell-bent-for-leather charge against Stuart's so-called Invincibles. Sweeping off his slouch hat and brandishing Spanish steel, he waved his troopers forward, first at a trot, then in a full gallop, shouting wildly: "Come on, boys! Give 'em the saber! Charge!"[13]

Later that afternoon, the young captain sauntered up to General Pleasonton and presented him with two batteries of captured Confederate horse artillery, a bevy of prisoners, and an elegant, gold-fringed, Southern Cross battle flag. Above crossed cannon barrels on sleek silk, it bore the inscription: *From the Ladies of Charlottesville to Stuart's Horse Artillery, Our Brave Defenders*.

As dusk began to settle over the battlefield, Pleasonton sighted rebel infantry on the march from Brandy Station. He recalled his forces and fell back the way he had come. With Pleasonton's orderly retirement, the greatest cavalry battle of the Civil War ended. The federals had lost 936 men, including 486 captured, compared to a Confederate total of 523. But Pleasonton made no secret of the great satisfaction he felt for the performance of his troopers, and he claimed a Union victory in the Battle of Brandy Station.

On the other side of the Rappahannock, Jeb Stuart

expressed equal or even greater delight at what his famed gray cavaliers had accomplished on the battlefield. Like his blue-coated rival, he too claimed victory. After all, even though twice surprised in a single day in his own bailiwick—to his singular embarrassment—he had held fast to his territory and had inflicted far more casualties than he had incurred.

The true victor at Brandy Station remains a subject for controversy. But none can deny that Stuart came away from the battle with a clear understanding that his adversaries were no longer the inept amateurs that he had faced during the first two years of the war. The Yankees had fought him hard and on equal terms. From now on, these veteran Union horsemen were going to make his job a lot tougher, and he must be prepared to meet their challenge. Robert E. Lee, his revered commander, had recently said it right: "We must all do more than formerly."[14]

Back at Union headquarters, General Hooker enthusiastically greeted Pleasonton and the flaxen-haired captain who had led an element of Buford's First Cavalry Brigade into action. "Captain," he said, shaking the young officer's hand and slapping him on the back, "you and General Pleasonton are to be complimented on the successful execution of my orders; and needless to say, I'm sure I'll have a great deal more for you to do in days to come."[15] The general could not have said it better.

Along with the praise of the general and many others, George Armstrong Custer afterward received still another citation for "gallantry throughout the fight."[16]

The Battle of Brandy Station marked the high point of the Confederate cavalry. For the rest of the war, its fortunes would steadily decline. The cavalry of both sides had acquitted themselves well in the opening battle of the Gettysburg campaign, but the greatest battle of the war remained to be fought three weeks later—outside a small town in Pennsylvania whose foremost claim to fame was its shoe factory.

A Nation Divided:
Secession and
Civil War

After the failure of Union Generals McClellan and Burnside to defeat Lee's determined armies, President Lincoln turned to Ulysses S. Grant (seen here riding hatless, at center). Grant rose to the occasion, and with generals like Sherman and Sheridan, helped turn the tide of the war in the Union's favor.

The origins of the Civil War—or the War Between the States, as Southerners prefer to call it—can be said to have originated with the founding of the United States of America. Although the root causes of the four-year conflict that tore the young nation apart from 1861 to 1865 were clearly evident in the 1820s and 1830s, they did not begin to pose a serious danger to national unity until the 1840s and 1850s. The principal divisive factors that threatened to separate the states of the North from those of the South were the related issues of slavery, trade and tariffs, and the doctrine of states' rights.

These issues evolved from the basic differences in their economies: a growing manufacturing sector supplemented by small farms using free labor in the northern states, compared to an agrarian economy of large farms (plantations) using slave labor in the southern states. A distinct difference in their interpretation of the U.S. Constitution added to the disharmony of North-South relations.

Northerners (and Westerners) favored a loose interpretation of the Constitution that would enable expanded federal power and thus government sponsorship of internal improvements—roads, railways, canals, and the like. Southerners opposed rapid development because it aided free-soil advocates and not the plantation owners. Trade tariffs protected manufacturers in the North but hindered large agricultural sales abroad (primarily cotton, tobacco, and sugar) by landholders in the South. Southerners therefore struggled to control trade and tariffs through the agency of strong states' rights.

Americans might have settled their differences over the issues of trade and tariffs and states' rights through the politics of compromise. On the issue of slavery, however, opinions on both sides became so opposite and unyielding, and emotions so enflamed, as to make it impossible for reasonable people to disagree in a reasonable way.

In the 1840s, antislavery advocates in the North sought to prohibit the spread of slavery to the Western territories that would eventually become new states. Slavery proponents in the South—fearing that northern attempts to limit slavery might ultimately jeopardize their own slaveholdings—opposed all efforts to block the westward spread of slavery. During the 1850s, some Northerners began demanding the abolition of slavery. Southerners responded by threatening to secede (withdraw) from the Union.

During the administration of President James Buchanan (1857-61), open warfare broke out in the Kansas Territory. Buchanan used federal troops to quiet the territory, but his army was too small and too scattered to curb

Slavery remained one of the most divisive issues leading to the Civil War. While issues of trade and states' rights may have been addressed by diplomatic means, slavery drove a deep wedge between northern and southern ideologies. This group of slaves was photographed outside their living quarters on a plantation on the Georgia sea islands.

further outbreaks of violence that were sure to follow. The battle lines of opposing viewpoints hardened fast. When Abraham Lincoln, the candidate of the antislavery Republican party, became president by a minority vote on November 6, 1860, South Carolina acted swiftly to carry out its threat to secede.

On December 20, South Carolina enacted an ordinance that declared "the union now subsisting between South

Carolina and other States, under the name of the 'United States of America,' is hereby dissolved."[17] Within six weeks, six additional slaveholding states in the South followed suit—Mississippi, Florida, Alabama, Georgia, Louisiana, and Texas. Following their secession, the seceding states met at Montgomery, Alabama, on February 8, 1861, and formed a new federation called the Confederate States of America (C.S.A.). The C.S.A. elected Jefferson Davis of Kentucky as their president nine days later. Davis, a graduate of West Point and hero of the Mexican War, had served in both houses of the U.S. Congress and as President Franklin S. Pierce's secretary of war.

The seven Confederate states immediately seized federal property within their borders, including military installations, except for Fort Pickens outside Pensacola and Fort Sumter in Charleston Harbor. The C.S.A. considered the U.S. government's retention of the two forts as equivalent to an act of war. Accordingly, President Davis called for a 100,000-man volunteer military force to serve for one year.

On March 4, 1861, Abraham Lincoln took the oath of office as the 16th President of the United States—which now consisted of 22 northern states, including three border states with divided loyalties. In his inaugural address, he declared that secession was illegal and that the seven secessionist states could not legally leave the United States on their own accord; legally, they still belonged to the Union. Pledging to retain the federal possessions in the South, he said, "The power confided in me will be used to hold, occupy and possess the property and places belonging to the government."[18] Fort Sumter clearly fell under this pronouncement.

After only a day in office, Lincoln received a request for troop reinforcements from Major Robert Anderson, federal commander of Fort Sumter, South Carolina. A few days after Lincoln's inauguration, Jefferson Davis, while

In this photograph, a print of which was later presented to him by the black community of Baltimore, President Lincoln stands with abolitionist Sojourner Truth, in commemoration of the Emancipation Proclamation, which called for the freeing of all slaves.

preparing for war, sent several emissaries to Washington D.C. to appeal for a swift Confederate takeover of Forts Sumter and Pickens. They returned to Montgomery with informal assurances that the forts would not be resupplied without proper notice. They expected an uneventful evacuation of Sumter.

Lincoln now faced a dilemma. Although Fort Sumter held no strategic value in case of war, to reinforce it might provide Davis with the provocation he needed to start a war. It might also drive eight more slaveholding states from the Union. Conversely, if he failed to meet Sumter's needs, enthusiasm for preserving the Union might dwindle among his constituents in the North. Worse yet, they might even come to accept the concept of a confederation south of the Mason-Dixon Line.

This line, defined by British surveyors Charles Mason and Jeremiah Dixon during 1765-68, marks the boundaries between the land grants of the Penns, proprietors of Pennsylvania, and the Baltimores, proprietors of Maryland. Originally, the Mason-Dixon Line represented the dividing line between the slaveholding states to its south and the free-soil states to its north. Latter-day Americans still regard it as the figurative boundary separating the South from the North.

Lincoln agonized over his Sumter dilemma for two weeks before deciding on March 29 to send supplies but no troops to the fort. He notified South Carolina governor Francis Pickens of his decision on April 8. The president still held hopes of avoiding war. Three days later, two Confederate officers arrived at Fort Sumter by boat under a white flag. They bore a message for fort commander Major Robert Anderson from Major General Pierre G. T. Beauregard, in charge of Charleston's defenses. It began: "I am ordered by the Government of the Confederate States to demand the evacuation of Fort Sumter."[19] Major Anderson respectfully declined to accommodate the general.

The American Civil War opened thunderously but bloodlessly. At 4:30 A.M. on April 12, 1861, Confederate gun batteries commenced firing on Fort Sumter. A reporter for the Charleston *Observer* noted: "Shell followed shell in quick

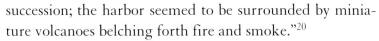

succession; the harbor seemed to be surrounded by minia-
ture volcanoes belching forth fire and smoke."[20]

Anderson's 90-man garrison returned fire and defended
the Union fort earnestly. But Sumter's guns could not match
the encircling fire from Beauregard's artillery. When
offered honorable terms after a 34-hour bombardment,
Anderson surrendered the federal fort, honoring his flag
with a 50-gun salute. The major and his troops were then
conveyed to a federal fleet outside Charleston Harbor for
further transportation to New York City.

The first militant act of the Civil War ended in a
Confederate victory without the death of a single soldier on
either side. Folks in Charleston and all over the South reacted
to the victory with a jubilance akin to ecstasy. A correspon-
dent for the London *Times* compared the streets of Charleston
to those of Paris after the French Revolution: "Crowds of
armed men singing and promenading the streets, the battle
blood running through their veins—that hot oxygen which
is called 'the flush of victory' on their cheeks . . . . Sumter
has set them distraught; never such a victory."[21]

President Lincoln responded to the Sumter attack by
calling for 75,000 volunteers to suppress what he perceived
as an insurrection. Surprisingly, 100,000 men answered
Lincoln's call. Less than three months later, when he
addressed a special session of Congress on July 4, 1861, the
ranks of the Union army had burgeoned to some 235,000
men. The somewhat amazed president said, "So large an
army as the government has now on foot, was never before
known." And he emphasized to members of the House and
Senate that every member of that force joined "of his own
free choice."[22]

Virginia, construing Lincoln's call to arms as an act of
war against the seceded states, itself seceded from the Union
on April 17. (The Confederates did *not* construe the seizure
of Fort Sumter to be an act of war. Rather, they regarded it

as the legitimate repossession of a property that rightfully belonged to South Carolina.) President Lincoln offered Colonel Robert E. Lee, a U.S. Army veteran, the opportunity to command the Union army the following day. But Lee, a loyal Virginian, declined and instead chose to become Jefferson Davis's military adviser.

When Virginia joined the new Confederacy, the C.S.A. moved its capital from Montgomery to the Virginian capital of Richmond and launched a remarkable recruitment program of its own. "Although its white population was only one-third that of the Union," write Civil War historians Gerald C. Henig and Eric Niderost, "it established an initial fighting force two-thirds as large."[23]

Meanwhile, Arkansas, Tennessee, and North Carolina quickly followed Virginia's lead and seceded from the Union. Eleven states now stood in open rebellion against the United States. And a state of war existed between Abraham Lincoln's North and Jefferson Davis's South.

At the start of the Civil War, the North enjoyed a distinct advantage in population, wealth, industry, mineral resources, and railways. The 1860 census reported the U.S. population at 31,443,321 persons, of which some 23,000,000 resided in the 22 northern states and about 9,000,000 in the 11 seceded states. The latter figure included 3,500,000 African-American slaves. But these numbers are deceptive. Since slaves performed labor that had to be done by free men in the North, the South was able to enlist into its armies a much higher proportion of its eligible white male population than the North.

With regard to wartime capital, estimates placed the wealth of the North at twice that of the South (excluding the slaves as property). Furthermore, the North boasted 90 percent of the nation's total manufacturing and controlled most of its mineral resources, whereas the agrarian South relied heavily on its cotton production.

Strategically, the North owned and maintained more than twice as many railroad miles as the South—22,000 miles to 9,000 miles. Ninety-six percent of American trains were manufactured in the North. The importance of railways cannot be overstated when considering that the Civil War was the first great war to use them as the principal means of conveying troops.

The North also had more and better ports and canals, and it retained most of the U.S. naval vessels as well as most of the privately owned merchant vessels. Lincoln wasted no time in exercising the Union's naval superiority. On April 18, 1861, he issued a proclamation "to set on foot a blockade of the ports"[24] from South Carolina to Texas. The president added Virginia and North Carolina eight days later.

Over the course of the war the armies of the North would field some 2,100,000 troops; those of the South, about 800,000 to 900,000. At peak strength, the armies of the North and the South would number about 1,000,000 and 600,000, respectively. The war aims of both sides were simple: The Confederacy hoped to confirm its independence; the Union wanted to reestablish its prewar status. These goals dictated their strategies. To validate its independence, the C.S.A. needed only to adopt a defensive posture, which, in turn, forced the North to take the offensive if it hoped to recover its lost territory.

Senator Robert Toombs of Georgia, in a parting speech to his Senate brethren, stated the Confederate stance this way: "You see the glittering bayonet and you hear the tramp of armed men from your capitol to the Rio Grande. Keep us in the Union by force? Come and do it! Georgia is on the warpath! We are ready to fight now."[25]

On July 8, 1861, Brigadier General P. G. T. Beauregard wrote, "If I could only get the enemy to attack me . . . I would stake my reputation on the handsomest victory that could be hoped for."[26] Thirteen days later the general got his wish. The first major battle of the war broke out at Manassas Junction, Virginia, 25 miles southwest of Washington D.C., behind a rambling river called Bull Run. Beauregard made good on his boast. With 30,000 Confederate troops, he repulsed 40,000 Union troops marching toward Richmond under Major General Irvin McDowell and sent them fleeing back toward Washington D.C.

Brigadier General Thomas J. Jackson's brigade of volunteers, many of them from the Virginia Military Institute, stood like statues in the face of whizzing bullets and fierce enemy attacks. Their rock-solid performance at the First Battle of Bull Run (or Manassas) earned their leader the nickname of "Stonewall" Jackson.

The stinging defeat at Bull Run galvanized the Union. Lincoln immediately called for a half-million more army recruits and assigned the task of commanding and training the new Department (later Army) of the Potomac to General George B. McClellan. A staunch Democrat, McClellan put aside politics and accepted the challenge. "The people call on me to save the country," he wrote, accurately if not humbly. "I must save it, and cannot respect anything that is in the way."[27] His plans to defeat the Confederacy were no less grandiose. When ready, he planned to invade Virginia by sea, seize Richmond, then move on to capture other major cities in the South.

Meanwhile, in the West (today's midwest), Brigadier General Nathaniel S. Lyon led a force of 5,400 Union troops into southwestern Missouri in an attempt to clear rebel troops from the area. On August 10, 1861, a C.S.A. force of 11,000 troops commanded by General Ben McCulloch defeated the much smaller Union force in a six-hour battle at Wilson's Creek. Union losses totaled 1,131 against 1,130 for the Confederates. Lyon took two rebel bullets before a third killed him. The Confederates remained a strong presence in southwestern Missouri, but Missouri remained in the Union.

The first major campaign of the war began in February 1862. Brigadier General Ulysses S. Grant's forces seized two Confederate strongholds in western Tennessee—Fort Henry on the Tennessee River and Fort Donelson on the Cumberland River. Grant's note demanding capitulation at Donelson revitalized dwindling enthusiasm for the war in the North: "No terms except an immediate and unconditional surrender can be accepted."[28] And his victories shifted the initiative in the West to the Union.

The Confederacy mounted a strong attempt to regain the initiative in Tennessee at Shiloh (Pittsburg Landing) in a bloody but inconclusive battle. After Shiloh, the rebel path in the West continued downhill, with a Union victory at New Madrid, Missouri, in March, and a drive on Corinth, Mississippi, in April—capped by Commodore David G. Farragut's capture of New Orleans on April 24. The loss of New Orleans, which proved to be irretrievable, represented a genuine disaster for the Southern cause. But even as the South's fortunes darkened in the West, they brightened by the day in the East.

In April, General McClellan launched his long-awaited Union offensive with the Army of the Potomac—about 100,000 troops—and started moving cautiously up the Virginia peninsula between the York and James rivers. His invasion of Virginia became known as the Peninsula Campaign and lasted about four months. The now-Confederate General Robert E. Lee and his able lieutenants, Major General T. J. "Stonewall" Jackson and Brigadier General Joseph E. Johnston, met McClellan. Their forces turned back the Union troops from Richmond for a second time during the Seven Days' Battles from June 25 to July 1, and the Peninsula Campaign ended in failure.

In late August, Lee ousted a second Union army from

Virginia, forcing the retreat of Brigadier General John Pope's newly formed Army of Virginia at the Second Battle of Bull Run. Lee then pressed northward into Maryland until checked by McClellan at Antietam (or Sharpsburg) in the bloodiest one-day battle of the war on September 17. The battle ended in a virtual standoff. But Lee elected to return to Virginia and regroup, and President Lincoln relieved McClellan for failing to pursue Lee.

On September 22, the president issued a preliminary document outlining his plans for emancipating runaway slaves. Lincoln wished "that all men every where could be free."[29] He also believed that stripping valuable labor from Southern plantations—but not from Northern farms—would cripple the Southern war effort. At the same time, it would provide an important manpower resource for the Union army. Lincoln signed the Emancipation Proclamation on the morning of January 1, 1863. The issuance of the official document freed all Southern slaves—and it served notice that the Union meant to suppress the Southern rebellion by any means possible.

Meanwhile, General Lee had regrouped his forces. On December 13, his Army of Northern Virginia delivered a crushing defeat to McClellan's successor, Major General Ambrose E. Burnside, and the Army of the Potomac, at Fredericksburg, Virginia, to close out the fighting in 1862.

In the aftermath of still another Union loss in the East, President Lincoln replaced Burnside as commander of the Army of the Potomac, installing Major General Joseph "Fighting Joe" Hooker in his stead. Hooker took the offensive in April 1863, attempting to outflank Lee's position at Chancellorsville, Virginia. The new Union leader declared with supreme confidence that he would pin Lee down, circle around him, and finish him off. Before the battle of May 1-5, Lincoln cautioned Hooker that the "hen is the wisest of all the animal creation because she never cackles until after the egg is laid."[30]

Lee sent Stonewall Jackson and 26,000 men around Hooker's right flank, while he held off his front with only 17,000 men against Hooker's 70,000. At the end of five days of savage fighting, it was Lee and his Confederates who found occasion to cackle. Lee's 60,000-man army delivered a ringing defeat to Hooker's 115,000-man army and forced Hooker to withdraw. But the thrill of victory was fleeting. Lee's most impressive victory cost him 12,000 casualties. Hooker lost 17,300.

For Lee, the saddest blow of all was the loss of a dear friend and comrade in arms. Stonewall Jackson was struck by a bullet in his left arm and doctors had to amputate it. When the news reached Lee, he said, "He has lost his left arm, but I have lost my right."[31] Jackson died on Sunday, May 10, from pneumonia resulting from his wound. Stonewall would be sorely missed. Lee had lost the one man he could not spare.

In the flush of triumph after Chancellorsville, Lee decided to pursue his initiative and cross the Mason-Dixon Line for a second incursion into the enemy's realm.

The Road to Gettysburg: Lee and Meade Move North

3

Lee's initial attempt to invade Northern soil at Antietam in 1862 ended with thousands of casualties, but no advance for the Confederate armies. Lee decided on a second invasion in 1863 at the Pennsylvania town of Gettysburg.

General Robert E. Lee's first incursion into Union territory had ended with a bloody clash and tactical stalemate at Antietam (or Sharpsburg) on September 17, 1862. The battle, often called the "bloodiest single day of the war,"[32] cost Lee 13,724 casualties (including 2,700 killed). His Union opponent, Major General George B. McClellan, incurred 12,140 casualties (including 2,108 killed). The standoff at Antietam Creek, near Sharpsburg, Maryland, forced Lee to withdraw to Confederate soil—a strategic defeat for his Army of Northern Virginia. (Strategy is the plan, or planning, for an entire operation of a war or campaign; tactics is the art of positioning or

The stalemate at Antietam resulted in the deaths of over 4,800 soldiers, Union and Confederate. After the battle, the corpses of men and horses littered the battlefield.

maneuvering forces skillfully in battle.) Lee, fresh off his victory over Major General Joseph Hooker's Army of the Potomac at Chancellorsville, decided in May 1963 that the time was at hand for a second invasion of the North. This time he expected to fare better.

General Lee planned to surmount his army's logistic (supply) problems by living off the land of his enemy. He could not hope to sustain his army on enemy soil indefinitely, of course, hence his planned second invasion of the North would in reality constitute only a raid on a grand scale. Even so, the possibility existed that a decisive Confederate victory might persuade the war-weary and success-starved Northern public to demand a peace settlement. Moreover, a resounding victory might also induce the British and the French to enter the war on the Confederate side. Such were Lee's thoughts in early June 1863, when he turned his army northward and started up the Shenandoah Valley, the long ravine separating the Allegheny and Blue Ridge Mountains in Virginia.

As a result of the subsequent cavalry clash at Brandy Station on June 9, General Hooker learned that Lee had more than just a raid in mind. Lee's whole army was on the move, except for Lieutenant General Ambrose P. Hill's newly formed Third Army Corps. Lee had left it in Fredericksburg to guard against a possible federal thrust across the river. Hooker wired the news to President Lincoln and proposed to move the Army of the Potomac south and across the Rappahannock River to launch a full-scale attack on Hill's lone corps. Hooker figured that he could easily overwhelm Hill's corps, or at least force Lee to return to help Hill. If Lee did not return to Fredericksburg, Hooker could vanquish Hill's corps and then move on to attack the Confederate capital of Richmond. Lincoln did not like the idea and overruled him.

The president and Major General Henry W. Halleck, the Union chief of staff, had repeatedly impressed upon Hooker the necessity of keeping the Army of the Potomac between Lee's main body and Washington D.C.

"In case you find Lee coming to the North of the Rappahannock," Lincoln wired back, "I would by no means cross to the south of it."[33] Though without previous military experience, the president possessed an uncanny grasp of battlefield strategy. He feared that Hill, fighting from entrenched positions, might put up a tougher fight than Hooker imagined.

Worse, if Hooker engaged Hill at Fredericksburg, Lee might conceivably hit his army from the rear, cutting the Army of the Potomac off from Washington D.C. and pinning it between two hostile forces. Lee's army could then hammer Hooker's army against Hill's anvil—a classic military maneuver. Or, as Lincoln put it, Hooker might find his army astraddle the Rappahannock "like an ox jumped half over a fence and liable to be torn by dogs front and rear, without a fair chance to gore one way or kick the other."[34]

Hooker next proposed a direct move on Richmond. Again the president overruled him. "If you had Richmond invested [surrounded] today," Lincoln responded, "you would not be able to take it in 20 days; meanwhile your communications, and with them your army, would be ruined. I think Lee's army, and not Richmond, is your true objective point."[35] In response, Hooker began shifting the Army of the Potomac toward Centreville, Virginia, on June 14, keeping it between Lee's army and Washington D.C. but choosing not to engage the Confederates while on the march.

At this time, the Army of Northern Virginia comprised three infantry corps and a cavalry division totaling about 75,000 men. In opposition, the Army of the Potomac consisted of seven infantry corps, a cavalry corps, and an artillery reserve (three brigades) numbering some 95,000 men in all. The two armies shared a common organization: A corps usually consisted of three divisions, each comprising two to four brigades; a brigade contained four to six regiments, numbering between 200 and 400 men each. Although the Confederates fielded fewer corps and divisions, these units were generally larger than those of the Union.

Despite the Union army's clear superiority in numbers, Hooker fretted about the losses he had sustained at Chancellorsville and their weakening effect on his army. Still, on June 14, he wired Lincoln: "If the enemy should be making for Maryland, I will make the best dispositions in my power to come up with him."[36]

On that same day, far to the northwest of Hooker, Lieutenant General Richard S. Ewell's Second Army Corps completed a rout of a Union garrison of 9,000 soldiers under Major General Robert H. Milroy at Winchester, in the lower Shenandoah Valley (during the Second Battle of Winchester, June 13-14, 1863). Ewell's action cleared the way for Lee's advance up the rest of the valley. Following the Battle of Brandy Station, Ewell's Corps had taken up position as the vanguard of Lee's northward move, while Jeb Stuart's cavalry screened Lee's flank, east of the Blue Ridge Mountains, and served as Ewell's "eyes." Along the way, Stuart's "Invincibles" renewed acquaintances with Pleasonton's cavalry in a string of skirmishes at Aldie, Middleburg, and Upperville.

In Washington D.C., Lincoln had foreseen a disastrous threat to Milroy and wanted more than assurances from Fighting Joe. When word of the Winchester rout reached the president, he wired a curt message to Hooker: "If the head of Lee's army is at Winchester and the tail at Fredericksburg, the animal must be very slim somewhere. Could you not break him?"[37]

"Impossible," Hooker replied, "I cannot divine his intentions as long as he fills the country with a cloud of cavalry." Fighting Joe concluded with a request that was to affect his future profoundly: "I am outnumbered. I need a reinforcement of 25,000 men."[38] The president denied his request. Hooker, disgruntled, kept his army in the vicinity of the Bull Run Mountains from June 17 to June 24th, exaggerating the size of the Confederate army and apparently reluctant to take on Lee without reinforcements.

By June 24, all of Lee's troops had crossed the Potomac and his lead elements had reached Chambersburg, Pennsylvania, while, amazingly, the entire Union army remained in Virginia. Also on the 24th, Hooker finally recognized that Lee could move between the Union army and Washington D.C. To preclude such a possibility, Hooker issued orders for his army to embark on a forced march north to Frederick, Maryland, which entailed covering distances of 20, 30, and 35 miles over the next three days. Under a blazing spring sun, hundreds of infantrymen succumbed to heatstroke and fell from the ranks. All the while, Hooker complained to Washington D.C. for reinforcements.

On June 27, at the end of a long march, Hooker felt frustrated because Army chief of staff Halleck would not allow him to transfer the garrison at Harper's Ferry, West Virginia, to his army. He fired off a bad-tempered note to Washington D.C.: "I must have more men. This is my resignation else."[39] The "else" prevailed. Halleck took Fighting Joe at his word—much to Hooker's surprise—and relieved him of command.

At 3:00 A.M. on June 28, Halleck's assistant adjutant general Colonel James A. Hardie awakened V Corps commander Major General George G. Meade at his field headquarters (H.Q.) near Frederick. Hardie handed the half-awake general a letter that said in part: "You will receive with this the order of the President placing you

In June 1863, General George Meade was given command of the Union's Army of the Potomac. Though surprised by the appointment, Meade moved his forces toward Gettysburg to check Lee's advance. He knew that a defeat on Union soil could lead to the loss of Baltimore, Washington, or even Philadelphia.

in command of the Army of the Potomac."[40] Meade could not believe his appointment, particularly since two of his six fellow corps commanders outranked him; even more so because he had no friends—political or otherwise—in high places who might help to advance his career. But now, for better or worse, the Army of the Potomac had a new commander on what clearly was the eve of battle.

History portrays General Meade as an intelligent, competent commander but not one of exceptional brilliance. Grizzled and short-tempered, he was a capable, determined subordinate. Although cautious, he had earned a reputation for tenacity, a character trait that would soon become very much in evidence. Halleck's instructions assured Meade of a free hand in discharging his new duties, which centered on the defense of Washington D.C. and Baltimore: "Should General Lee move upon either of these places, it is expected that you will either anticipate him or arrive with him so as to give him battle."[41] Halleck also directed him to use the garrison at Harper's Ferry to his best advantage, the use of which he had previously denied to Hooker.

Meade, even as he grappled with all the burdensome details of a new command, issued orders for his army to resume its northward march on June 29. He intended to move within striking distance of Lee's flank. When Lee learned of Meade's appointment, he reportedly said, "General Meade will commit no blunder in my front, and if I make one he will hasten to take advantage of it."[42] Lee, though unaware of it then, had already committed a serious blunder.

Several days earlier, Jeb Stuart, having successfully screened the passes through the Blue Ridge Mountains for Lee's army, dispatched a message to Lee requesting orders for the next phase of the campaign. The next day, June 23, Lee replied:

> If you find that he [the enemy] is moving northward, and that two brigades can guard the Blue Ridge & take care of your rear, you can move with the other three into Maryland & take position on General Ewell's right, place yourself in communication with him, guard his flank, keep him informed of the enemy's movements & collect all the supplies you can for use of the army.[43]

Lee's response to Stuart turned out to be one of the most controversial orders ever issued by the Confederate commander. Although Stuart's primary task of screening Lee's infantry and providing Ewell with intelligence remained unchanged, Lee had neglected to limit Stuart to a specific itinerary. Lee was known for providing his commanders with a broad understanding of what he wanted and relying on their individual initiative to work out the details. In the days ahead, Lee's lack of specificity would leave him blinded to the movements of Meade's army for much of the campaign.

Lee undoubtedly expected Stuart to ride along the west side of the Blue Ridge, where he would continue to screen the army, keep track of Union movements, and serve as his eyes and ears. But his orders did not specifically state his expectations. Stuart, who had twice before introduced himself to fame and glory by way of daring raids around the federal army, decided to try it again. Some say that his less than stellar performance at Brandy Station and again at Upperville might have stirred in him an impulse to recapture some of the grandeur he had known earlier.

On June 25, irrespective of his motivation, Stuart left two brigades to guard the passes through the Blue

Ridge. With his three other brigades, he rode south, around the tail of the federal army, then northward, keeping to the east of Meade. Lee did not hear from him again for a week. Throughout the week, Lee would ask of all comers, "Can you tell me where General Stuart is?"[44] But none could, and Lee continued north without benefit of the eyes and ears that had served him so well in the past. To the best of his knowledge, the Army of the Potomac was still in Virginia.

Three days later, on the 28th, Lee received a report from a Confederate spy that the federal army had crossed the Potomac and was now concentrated near Frederick, Maryland. That next day, Meade began to move cautiously northward toward the small Pennsylvania town of Gettysburg. The 47-year-old Meade, a veteran soldier, recognized that a defeat in Union territory could mean the loss of Baltimore, Washington D.C., and even Philadelphia. He planned to check Lee's advance and engage his forces at a time and place yet undecided.

Lee, on the other hand, realized the vulnerability of his scattered army. He had intended to concentrate his forces near Harrisburg, Pennsylvania. But unless he could draw his strung-out troops together quickly— Ewell's corps had already reached Carlisle on June 27— Meade's advancing army might defeat his own a piece at a time. Lee immediately changed his plans and ordered his army to concentrate near Cashtown, nine miles west of Gettysburg. He chose Cashtown to ensure that the imminent conflict would take place east of the Blue Ridge Mountains.

This location would allow him room to maneuver and expedite his supplies from Virginia. Given Meade's defeat, it would also serve as an excellent base from which to launch a new advance against key strategic objectives in the North. Conversely, in case of his own

After Gettysburg, the defeat of the South was slow in coming. In the two years of battle that followed, Union General Philip Henry Sheridan and his cavalry laid waste to the rich Shenandoah Valley of Virginia.

Union Order of Battle at Gettysburg

ARMY OF THE POTOMAC

Commander
Major General George G. Meade

I Corps
Major General John F. Reynolds
Major General Abner Doubleday

II Corps
Major General Winfield S. Hancock
Brigadier General John Gibbon

III Corps
Major General Daniel E. Sickles
Major General David B. Birney

V Corps
Major General George Sykes

VI Corps
Major General John Sedgwick

XI Corps
Major General Oliver O. Howard

XII Corps
Major General Henry W. Slocum

Cavalry Corps
Major General Alfred Pleasonton

Artillery Reserve
Brigadier General Robert O. Tyler

Confederate Order of Battle at Gettysburg

ARMY OF NORTHERN VIRGINIA

Commander
General Robert E. Lee

First Army Corps
Lieutenant General James Longstreet

Second Army Corps
Lieutenant General Richard S. Ewell

Third Army Corps
Lieutenant General Ambrose P. Hill

Cavalry
Stuart's Division
Major General J. E. B. Stuart

Imboden's Command
Brigadier General John D. Imboden

defeat, the mountains would aid his withdrawal back into Virginia.

At this point, neither Lee nor Meade had thought much about Gettysburg. Each commander intended to occupy a strong defensive position and force the other to attack. It was the network of roads converging on Gettysburg that attracted thousands of marching feet in the last days of June 1863 and ultimately determined the site of the most famous battle of the Civil War.

No fewer than 10 roads led into the small Pennsylvania town of 2,400 people, the seat of Adams County. Like spokes to a wheel hub, they centered on Gettysburg: from Mummasburg, Carlisle, and Heidlersburg to the north; from York and Hanover to the east; from Baltimore, Taneytown, and Emmitsburg to the south; and from Hagerstown and Chambersburg to the west. On June 30, a Confederate infantry brigade under Brigadier General James J. Pettigrew approached Gettysburg from the west along the Chambersburg Pike. At about the same time, a division of Union cavalry led by Brigadier General John Buford advanced on the town from the south over the Emmitsburg Road.

Buford's cavalry, the advance guard of Meade's army, cantered into Gettysburg at about 11 that morning. Buford and his troopers had been scouring the countryside for signs of Lee's army. They found the town in "a terrible state of excitement."[45] The excited townspeople told Buford that a mess of rebel infantry had just left, up the Chambersburg Pike to the northwest. Buford, whose troops were "fagged out"[46] after several days in the saddle, decided to halt for the night. But he sent out two brigades to scout the areas to the north and west.

Buford's scouts returned late that night to confirm a Confederate presence on the Chambersburg Pike. Buford hastily sent word of his location and findings to Meade's headquarters at Taneytown, Maryland. He also sent a message to Major General John F. Reynolds, commander of I Corps. Positioned about 11 miles to the south at Emmitsburg, I Corps was the closest Union infantry unit.

Unknown to Buford and his scouts, however, Lieutenant General Ambrose P. Hill's entire Confederate Third Army Corps was encamped near Cashtown, less than a day's march away. Worse yet, Lieutenant General Richard S. Ewell's Second Army Corps was moving

south from Carlisle. A rebel vise—about 50,000 troops—
was closing fast on Buford's overmatched cavalry. No
matter the mismatch, their job now was to stand in place
until help arrived. On a sultry summer night in June, the
greatest battle of the Civil War was set to begin.

July 1: Chance
Encounter

The Battle of Gettysburg represents a prime example of what battle buffs call a "meeting engagement" or an "encounter battle," which simply means an accidental battle resulting from a chance encounter. Given a choice, neither Lee nor Meade would have chosen this town—whose main attraction was a shoe factory— as the site for a major confrontation. It just happened. When the two armies met, all roads led to Gettysburg. In Lee's words, "A battle thus became, in a measure, unavoidable."[47]

Both Lee and Meade had originally intended to seek a strong defensive position and force the other to attack. Prior to the battle, Meade had planned on establishing a potential defensive line along Big Pipe Creek, some 20 miles south of Gettysburg. Lieutenant

General James Longstreet, First Army Corps commander and one of Lee's chief lieutenants, also favored a defensive stance. He recommended deploying the Army of Northern Virginia defensively between the Army of the Potomac and Washington D.C., thereby compelling Meade to attack. But Lee, who had vowed earlier not to "assume a tactical offensive, but to force his antagonist to attack him,"[48] changed his mind and decided to attack the enemy at Gettysburg. Military analysts rank this decision among the most controversial of Lee's career.

Critical military decisions invariably must take into account two vital factors: the terrain and the situation. In Lee's situation, Meade's forces outnumbered his own by about 25,000 men. Moreover, the terrain at Gettysburg heavily favored a defensive posture.

The town itself lay on low ground between two small streams, Rock Creek and Willoughby's Run, which formed the eastern and western tributaries of the Monocacy River. A seam of high ground called Seminary Ridge (for the Lutheran seminary located on it) rose just west of town, running approximately north and south. Moving westward, McPherson's Ridge stood between Seminary Ridge and Willoughby's Run and ran parallel to both. Farthest to the west stood Herr Ridge, across the Run and parallel to it.

A shorter spur called Cemetery Ridge ran in about the same direction south of town, with Cemetery Hill, its commanding height, located at its northern end. The spur ended about three miles south of town. Three-quarters of a mile west of the southern tip of Cemetery Hill lay a peach orchard, a wheat field, and a rugged, rocky patch known as "Devil's Den." Two detached hills south of Cemetery Hill have withstood the test of time with the unlikely names of Little Round Top and Round Top.

Rounding out some of the principal terrain features, Culp's Hill loomed over the low ground about a half-mile east of Cemetery Hill, adjacent to Rock Creek. And Power's Hill stood a mile south of Culp's Hill.

On the eve of battle, both armies were on the march and advancing on Gettysburg from five directions. That night, more than 70,000 troops laid out their bed rolls within 10 miles of the little town. Meade established his headquarters at Taneytown, Maryland, 10 miles southeast of Gettysburg, while Lee spent the night at Greenwood, 10 miles east of Chambersburg.

Lee felt determined not to engage the federal army until he had fully reassembled his own army and could garner more specific information as to the strength, location, and intent of the federal forces. He had issued explicit orders to his corps commanders—A. P. Hill, in particular—that he wanted no "general engagement."[49] Only that morning, Brigadier General James J. Pettigrew had led his First Brigade toward Gettysburg in search of badly needed shoes. But when he encountered Buford's cavalry pickets (sentries) west of town, Pettigrew withdrew in compliance with Lee's order not to engage the enemy until his entire army arrived on the scene.

That night, however, Pettigrew's divisional commander, Major General Henry Heth, reported the incident to Third Army Corps commander Lieutenant General A. P. Hill. Pettigrew insisted that the federal cavalry represented a formidable force. But Hill and Heth both concluded that Buford's cavalry was more likely only a reconnaissance patrol and that only a small militia defended the town. They both thought that Meade was still in Maryland. And the need to acquire shoes remained critical. Heth said that he would like to take his division into Gettysburg the next day and get those shoes, assuming that Hill did not have any objections. "None in the world,"[50] Hill told him.

In this way, Lee's commanders let him down. And

The many roads leading into the small Pennsylvania town allowed troops, weapons, and supplies to be shipped in easily. The result was three days of relentless battle that saw more than 10,000 casualties per day on the field.

the Battle of Gettysburg began the next morning as a chance encounter.

Heth's division, along with a battalion of artillery, started marching down the Chambersburg Pike at 5:00 A.M., followed by Major General William D. Pender's division, also accompanied by a battalion of artillery. Of the brigade commanders' disdain for the enemy forces, Lieutenant Louis B. Young, Pettigrew's aide, later wrote, "This spirit of unbelief had taken such hold, that I doubt if any of the commanders of brigades, except General Pettigrew, believed that we were marching to battle, a weakness on their part which rendered them unprepared for what was about to happen."[51] Unbelief quickly turned to belief. Buford was prepared.

Buford had expected the Confederates to return in force on the morning of July 1. The night before, he had told his brigade commanders, "They will attack you in the morning and they will come booming—skirmishers [advance elements deployed without any organized formations] three-deep. You will have to fight like the devil until supports arrive."[52] If anything, Buford had understated the events as they were soon to transpire.

Accordingly, Buford positioned Colonel William Gamble's First Brigade of cavalry to the west of Gettysburg and Colonel Thomas C. Devin's Second Brigade to the north and northwest, the most likely avenues of approach. To provide early warning, Buford set in a line of pickets (sentries) along Whisler's (now Knoxlyn) Ridge, near Marsh Creek. Once under attack, the pickets were to fall back to Herr Ridge and join a larger body of cavalry assigned to fight a delaying action for as long as possible. This body, when it could no longer withstand the enemy assault, would then retire to Buford's main line of defense on McPherson's Ridge—or, if necessary, even to Seminary Ridge.

On Whisler's Ridge, troopers of the Eighth Illinois Cavalry occupied vedette (mounted picket) post number one, about three-quarters of a mile east of where Marsh Creek crosses the Chambersburg Pike. The pickets sighted the first of Heth's columns kicking up dust on the Pike at about 7:00 A.M. They sent for their sergeant, Levi S. Shafer, who joined them, soon followed by their commander, Lieutenant Marcellus E. Jones. At about 7:30 A.M., Jones borrowed Shafer's carbine and fired off a round at a

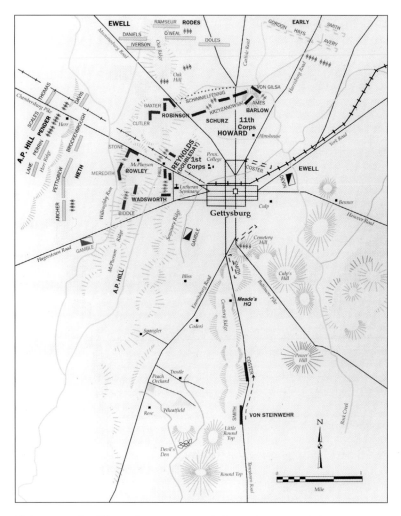

This map of military forces around Gettysburg on July 1, 1863 shows Union forces defending the western approach to the town. Confederate forces advancing from the west engaged Union troops in a bloody battle, forcing the Union armies to retreat to Cemetery Hill and Culp's Hill.

Confederate on horseback. His shot, which probably missed, is generally considered to have been the first shot fired at Gettysburg. The fighting began shortly afterward.

At 8:00 A.M., Heth's division began advancing on Gamble's pickets on Whisler's Ridge, slowly forcing them back eastward to Herr's Ridge, but not before the dismounted cavalrymen fought a textbook delaying action. A lieutenant in the Eighth Illinois described the initial action this way:

> The enemy advanced slowly and carefully . . . . Our first position proved to be well taken. Scattering my men to the right and left at intervals of 30 feet and behind posts and rail fences . . . I directed them to throw their carbines sights up for 800 yards . . . . We gave the enemy the benefit of long-range practice . . . . The firing was rapid from our carbines, and induced the belief of four times the number actually present.[53]

Contrary to the popular view of cavalry fighting— thundering hooves and flashing sabers—Buford's troopers usually fought on foot, using their horses primarily as a fast way of reaching the battlefield. Once there, they would dismount, assign one man in four to hold the horses in the rear, then fight as infantry. Armed with breech-loading Sharps carbines, which could be loaded far faster than the muzzle-loading rifles carried by all infantry troops, the Union cavalrymen could generate the fire-power of several times their number.

By 9:30 A.M., Heth's Confederates had forced Gamble's cavalrymen off Herr's Ridge and back to Buford's main defense line on McPherson's Ridge. Heth then deployed his two lead brigades—Brigadier General Joseph Davis's to the left and Brigadier General James Archer's to the right—and they began an assault on McPherson's Ridge, with 20 cannon backing their attack. Heth held his other two brigades—Pettigrew's and Colonel John Brockenbrough's—in reserve.

On the ridge and awaiting their attack, Buford had positioned Gamble's 1,700 troopers and one regiment of

Devin's brigade, supported by Lieutenant John Calef's six-gun battery of horse artillery. Heth's forces totaled about 7,000 men, which gave him roughly a four-to-one advantage over Buford's troops, who were, more to their disadvantage, spread thinly over an extended area. In their favor, the federal firepower equaled that of nearly 6,000 men, and the horse soldiers used it judiciously. Still, against such odds, no one could expect them to hold out for very long.

Buford watched his men defend their ground heroically from his vantage point in the cupola of the Lutheran seminary, no doubt wondering what was keeping the arrival of Major General John F. Reynolds's I Corps. Much to Buford's relief, Reynolds galloped up to the seminary about 9:45 A.M. After surveying Buford's positions, Reynolds decided that the area was a suitable place to engage Lee's army and fired off a message to Meade: "I will fight them inch by inch, and if driven into the town I will barricade the streets and hold them as long as possible."[54]

Reynolds returned to his corps south of town and rushed it forward, arriving at 10:15 A.M. They joined the battle just in time to prevent two Confederate infantry brigades (Archer and Davis) from overrunning Buford's forces on McPherson's Ridge. Reynolds immediately deployed the Second Maine artillery battery under Captain James A. Hall, which suppressed one of Heth's batteries on Herr's Ridge, 1,300 yards away, while Brigadier General Lysander Cutler's Second Brigade formed into the line. Brigadier General Solomon Meredith's First Brigade—the storied "Iron Brigade" of Midwestern troops that had distinguished itself at Antietam—filled in the line to their left, as its band played "Yankee Doodle Dandy." The two brigades comprised the First Division of I Corps, led by Brigadier General James S. Wadsworth.

Suddenly, a swarm of Archer's infantry charged the

western slope of the ridge and unleashed a tremendous volley at the Second Wisconsin, Meredith's lead element. Reynolds, seeing many of their men topple and their ranks start to waver, rode up on his "powerful black horse" and shouted, "Forward men, forward for God's sake, and drive those fellows out of the woods."[55]

An instant later, a minié ball struck him in the neck. Reynolds reeled off his horse and tumbled to the ground—dead. (A minié ball is a soft lead conical bullet with a hollow base used in muzzle-loading firearms.) Reynolds had arrived in time to fend off a Union defeat for the moment, but the battle's outcome would depend on the actions of others. Command of I Corps devolved (passed on) to Third Division commander Major General Abner Doubleday. Under Doubleday's leadership, the Union forces succeeded in beating back Heth's advance brigades and forcing them to withdraw to Herr's Ridge.

Archer's brigade fell apart during the withdrawal and Union troops took 75 prisoners, including Archer himself, who was seized by a private in the Second Wisconsin and marched to the rear. Along the way, Archer encountered Doubleday, whom he had known at West Point. Doubleday extended his hand and smiled pleasantly. "Good morning, Archer. How are you?" he said. "I am glad to see you."[56]

Archer declined the handshake with a scowl and said, "Well, I am not glad to see you, by a damned sight, Doubleday."[57]

A lull then settled over the battlefield as both sides brought up reinforcements. Heth (and in turn Hill) had missed a grand opportunity to score a stunning victory over the Yankees by not committing his other two brigades—Pettigrew and Brockenbrough—when they might have overwhelmed the defenders on McPherson's Ridge. Heth now pulled back Archer's broken brigade and brought up Pettigrew's and Brockenbrough's to shore up Davis's brigade. At the same time, Hill sent Dorsey Pender's division to Heth's support. Some 15,000 Confederates now faced Doubleday, who felt grateful to welcome the appearance of the remaining two divisions of I Corps—the Second and Third, under Brigadier Generals John C. Robinson and Thomas A. Rowley, respectively. Their arrival boosted the Union numbers to about 8,500 men, plus Buford's cavalry.

Amid bursting shells, Major General Oliver P. Howard's XI Corps joined the fray at noon and Howard assumed field command. First off, he climbed the belfry of the Lutheran seminary and viewed the surrounding area. Every road from north and west surged with a stream of gray-clad troops marching toward Gettysburg. He perceived the greatest immediate danger to be streaming in from the north. Howard was observing the arrival of Major General Robert E. Rodes's division and Major General Jubal A. Early's division—a total of 15,000 troops. The two divisions formed a part of Lieutenant General Richard S. Ewell's Confederate Second Army Corps, now doubling back from Carlisle and York.

Howard turned XI Corps over to Major General Carl Schurz, his senior division commander, and ordered him to deploy two divisions of XI Corps, about 6,000 men, at right angles to Doubleday north of town. The Union defense line now formed a lazy L facing west and north. Howard used Buford's cavalry to protect the flanks and held a third division in reserve at his headquarters on Cemetery Hill. His defensive strategy was simple: Delay the enemy long enough for Meade to arrive with the rest of the Army of the Potomac.

Meanwhile, Confederate commander Robert E. Lee arrived at Hill's headquarters at about 2:00 P.M. By then, three Confederate divisions had been locked in combat with elements of two Union corps for six hours—24,000 Grays against 19,000 Blues. Lee did not like the way the battle appeared to be going. From Herr's Ridge, he observed that the action constituted more than a skirmish. He had exerted every effort to avoid a general engagement until his army was reunited and until he could learn more of the terrain and his opponent's strength. "I cannot think what has become of Stuart," he said. "I ought to have heard from him long before now. He may have met with disaster, but I hope not."[58]

About then, Heth rode up. Eager to make amends for his less than impressive showing to that point, he requested permission of Lee to return to the attack. Lee replied, "No, I am not prepared to bring on a general engagement today. Longstreet is not up."[59] Still in the Shenandoah Valley, Longstreet's corps was due to arrive that evening. But fate soon overrode Lee's judgment. Rodes's division arrived at Oak Hill—north of McPherson's Ridge and the Mummasburg Road—even while they spoke and attacked the right flank of I Corps (Robinson).

Heth returned to the attack at 2:30 P.M., this time with the brigades of Pettigrew and Brockenbrough—about 3,500 men. A Union colonel on McPherson's Ridge observed their advance and later wrote:

> They marched along quietly and with confidence, but swiftly. I watched them . . . and am confident that when they advanced they outflanked us at least half a mile on our left. . . . There was not a shadow of a chance of our holding this ridge.[60]

The colonel called it right. Doubleday's bluecoats tried anyway. The action raged fiercely all along the lazy L, but none surpassed the fighting in the I Corps area for pure savagery. The Nineteenth Indiana and Twenty-Fourth Michigan regiments traded lethal volleys with the Eleventh and Twenty-Sixth North Carolina regiments at ranges of 40 yards or less. Colonel Samuel Williams of the Nineteenth

Indiana told his men, "Hold our colors on this line, or lie here under them."[61] Many tried that afternoon, but the weight of numbers prevailed.

The rebels finally drove the Yankees off the ridge about 3:30 P.M., and I Corps withdrew farther eastward to Seminary Ridge. After the fight for McPherson's Ridge, one veteran of the Twenty-Sixth North Carolina surveyed the awful cost of winning: "[The] ground was gray with dead and disabled,"[62] All around the hillside, his fellow survivors searched the bodies of fallen comrades for desperately needed cartridges.

At this juncture, Pender's fresh troops passed through the ranks of Heth's fatigued soldiers and pressed the attack against I Corps, forcing Doubleday's corps—now reduced from 8,200 to 2,500 men—to continue its retreat through town. Doubleday took refuge on the heights of Cemetery Hill, south of town.

Meanwhile, to the north of town, XI Corps was experiencing similar difficulties. While Rodes was still battling Robinson's division, Early's division (Ewell) arrived from York about 3:30 P.M. Brigadier General John B. Gordon's Georgia brigade assailed Schurz's exposed right flank, held only briefly by Brigadier General Francis C. Barlow's division. When the Georgians wounded and captured Barlow himself, his troops fled, rallied only briefly at the Alms House on the Harrisburg Road, then broke and ran again. Rodes then joined Early and entered Gettysburg from the north, while XI Corps exited in the south.

Earlier, when news of the death of Reynolds had reached Meade, he immediately sent Major General Winfield Scott Hancock to take over field command at Gettysburg. Hancock arrived just as the Union survivors started streaming out of town. He and Howard, disappointed at having been relieved, set to work laying out new defenses on Cemetery Hill and later on nearby Culp's Hill, digging in and installing artillery. Hancock instilled new spirit into his battle-drained troops with his own cheerful energy. At 5:00 P.M., the arrival of the lead elements of Major General Henry W. Slocum's XII Corps further enhanced their spirits. Pleased with the dramatic turn-around of his revitalized troops and the strength of his hastily prepared defenses, Hancock reported to Meade that his position "cannot well be taken."[63] It appears that Early felt likewise.

A half-hour earlier, Lee, observing the action from his new position on Seminary Ridge, had begun to sense that a decisive victory might be possible. He asked A. P. Hill if his men could once more muster enough strength to push up and over Cemetery Hill. Neither Heth's nor Pender's troops, Hill replied, had an ounce of energy left in them. Lee then sent aide Major Walter Taylor to instruct Ewell, north of town, to press ahead and capture Cemetery Hill "if practicable."[64]

Lee's proviso left the decision to Ewell. After viewing the federal defenses, by then bristling with cannon, and unaware of what other federal forces might pose a threat to his left flank, Ewell opted not to attack. Critics and apologists of his decision still debate whether it resulted in a lost opportunity for a decisive Confederate victory at a rare time when the South held a numerical advantage. The argument remains unresolved.

In any event, when night fell over the battlefield, Lee held a clear advantage. Union losses numbered slightly more than 9,000, including about 3,000 captured; Confederate casualties totaled about 6,000. But Union forces still controlled the high ground south of town, and help was rushing to their aid. The chance encounter at the little Pennsylvania town of Gettysburg was about to turn into a general engagement.

Little Round Top was a hill that formed the anchor of the Union's left flank at Gettysburg. Left almost unprotected, the hill gave Confederate forces a chance to outflank Union forces. General Joshua Chamberlain took the offensive, and by securing Little Round Top, turned the battle in the Union's favor.

July 2: Great Hearts on Little Round Top

Although General Robert E. Lee had not planned the battle the way it happened, he now had a general engagement on his hands—ready or not. Throughout the night, Confederate and Union forces poured onto the battlefield.

Union commander Major General George G. Meade left Taneytown about 10:00 P.M. and joined his forces south of Gettysburg around midnight. Three of Meade's corps commanders greeted his arrival at Cemetery Hill. They all agreed that the Union-held ground was a good place for a fight. A saddle-weary Meade replied, "I am glad to hear you say so, gentlemen, for it is too late to leave it."[65] He then surveyed Cemetery Ridge and its surrounds to check its defenses.

Remounting, Meade rode slowly through the clustered forms of sleeping soldiers, down Cemetery Ridge to the base of Little Round Top. Backtracking to Cemetery Hill, he then ascended Culp's Hill on the extreme right. The Union positions, he learned, resembled the shape of a fishhook, anchored on Culp's Hill and Cemetery Hill, then curving southward and extending down Cemetery Ridge to the two detached hills known as Little Round Top and Round Top.

During his inspection tour, Meade observed the positioning of his defenses. Culp's Hill, the barb of the hook and anchor of the Union right flank, was manned by Slocum's newly arrived XII Corps on the eastern side of the hill and the remainder of Wadsworth's division (I Corps) on the northern side. Howard's XI Corps occupied Cemetery Hill to the west. The remnant of I Corps, now under the command of Major General John Newton, held the northern part of Cemetery Ridge. (Meade had ordered Newton forward from Major General John Sedgwick's VI Corps—still en route and not expected to arrive until late afternoon—because he mistrusted Doubleday.)

To Newton's left, Hancock's II Corps deployed south along the ridge. Rising no more than 12 feet higher than the ground in front of it, Cemetery Ridge hardly dominated the terrain, but it offered a clear field of fire to Hancock's troops. Major General Daniel E. Sickle's III Corps filled in the rest of the ridge, stopping just short of the Round Tops at this time. All along the line, the Union troops faced west toward their adversaries who looked east from Seminary Ridge.

Meade completed his tour at sunrise, feeling confident that his forces could hold position. He had ample reason to feel optimistic. His forces now constituted 51 brigades (1,500-2,000 men each) of infantry, backed by seven cavalry brigades and 354 guns (cannon). Along the three-mile perimeter of the "fishhook," the density of federal soldiers equaled 15 defenders for every yard of front held.

By contrast, the main body of Confederates facing them, fanned out in a crescent-shaped posture along Seminary Ridge, could muster only six men to the yard. Overall, against Meade's Army of the Potomac, Lee's Army of Northern Virginia could field only 34 infantry brigades (1,500-3,000 men each), supported by one cavalry brigade and 272 guns. Although Confederate units tended to run larger than their Union counterparts, Lee still ended up with about a 20,000-man disadvantage. Yet, he did not act as an underdog.

Lee's position roughly flanked the southern approaches to Gettysburg. From west to east, respectively, Hill's Third Corps held a line along Seminary Ridge that extended north to town and through it, while Ewell's Second Corps wrapped around Cemetery and Culp's Hills and threatened them from the northeast. Lee's lines fell outside Meade's and stretched for about four miles, affording Meade the added advantage of interior lines that enabled the shifting of men and equipment over shorter distances in quicker time.

As two divisions of Longstreet's First Army Corps arrived on July 2, they extended Lee's right flank along Seminary Ridge to a position opposite Little Round Top. Longstreet himself had arrived on the ridge late the previous afternoon, where he found Lee scanning the federal positions with field glasses. Longstreet also took a look, then turned to Lee and declared, "All we have to do is throw our army around their left, and we shall interpose between the federal army and Washington . . . The federals will be sure to attack us."[66] Lee differed.

Confederate General James Longstreet tried unsuccessfully to dissuade Lee from attacking Union forces at their center, suggesting instead an approach from the Union's left. Longstreet's delay in reaching his position allowed Union General Meade the time he needed to strengthen his defenses.

"No," said the Confederate commander, "the enemy is there, and I am going to attack him there."[67] Longstreet, who remembered seeing Lee's army slaughter thousands of federals from behind stone walls in the Battle of Fredericksburg, tried to dissuade Lee but to no avail. Lee had made up his mind. Many critics believe that his decision to attack doomed the Confederacy. Lee later justified his actions in his report on Gettysburg:

> I had not intended to deliver a general battle so far from our base unless attacked, but coming unexpectedly upon the whole Federal Army, to withdraw through the mountains with our extensive [supply] trains would have been difficult and dangerous. At the same time we were unable to await an attack, as the country was unfavorable for collecting supplies in the presence of the enemy.[68]

Early on July 2, Lee laid his battle plan before his commanders individually. (He never assembled them in a group, which invited later misunderstandings and confusion.) Simply stated, two divisions of Longstreet's corps of fresh troops—Major Generals Lafayette McLaw's and John B. Hood's—were to attack Meade's southern flank near the Round Tops. (Major General George E. Pickett's division of Longstreet's corps had been left at Chambersburg to guard wagon trains.) At the sound of the guns, Ewell's corps of battle-worn troops was to launch a diversionary attack on Culp's and Cemetery Hills from the northeast.

Meanwhile, two divisions of Hill's corps, weakened by the previous day's battle, were to hold the Union troops in the center of the line by feigning an attack. Hill's fresh division, under Major General Richard H. Anderson, would then storm Cemetery Hill. If the battle went well, Lee's army would ensnare Meade's in a classic pincer movement—a double envelopment in which one army converges on another from two sides.

Lee planned to open his attack at 11:00 A.M. But because of a combination of delays in moving troops into preattack positions, coupled with Longstreet's clear lack of enthusiasm for Lee's strategy, Longstreet did not attack until 4:00 P.M. (Some of his detractors believe that Longstreet lagged intentionally, possibly hoping that Meade would attack first. Such speculation remains unsubstantiated.)

The delay suited Meade just fine. He used the extended lull to strengthen his defenses. Unknown to him, however, III Corps commander Sickles, seeking to improve his position at the south end of Cemetery Ridge, shifted his corps forward about 3:30 P.M. to some slightly higher ground crowned by a peach orchard. In so doing, he created a salient—a bulge—in the Union lines, thereby exposing his flanks to attack.

When Sickles reported his movement to General Meade at the latter's H.Q. in the Leister House, at the northeast end of Cemetery Ridge, Meade fumed and rode off down the ridge with Sickles to examine the unauthorized salient. Sickles tried to justify his shift to higher ground, but Meade would have none of it.

"General Sickles," he countered, "this is in some respects higher ground than that of the rear, but there is still higher in front of you, and if you keep on advancing you will find constantly higher ground all the way to the mountains."[69] Sickles offered to pull back at once but his skirmishers had already entered into incidental contact with the enemy.

"Too late," Meade snapped. "You must fight it out where you are; I'll move troops at once to support you."[70] Meade ordered Major General George Sykes's recently arrived V Corps and a division of Hancock's II Corps to fill the gap between III and II Corps.

Just about then, Brigadier General John W. Geary's Second Division of XII Corps, assigned to occupy the south end of Cemetery Ridge and the Round Tops until the arrival of III Corps, marched off to rejoin XII Corps on Culp's Hill. The departure of Geary and the failure of Sickles to occupy the Round Tops left the vital hills uncovered—unknown to Meade—except for a smattering of signal corps personnel. And at 4:00 P.M., the sound of cannons heralded the start of Longstreet's attack.

Meade, while still chastising Sickles, ordered Brigadier General Gouverneur K. Warren, his chief engineer, to check on the security of Little Round Top, the anchor of the Union left flank. "Warren! I hear a little peppering going on in the direction of that little hill off yonder," he said. "I wish that you would ride over and if anything serious is going on . . . attend to it."[71] A short ride to a little hill was to earn Warren a small place in American history.

Warren, to his astonishment, found on the key hill only a few signalmen preparing to leave. And from the crest, he could see gray-clad troops approaching. Meade's engineer recognized at once that the little hill held "the key of the whole position."[72] The loss of Little Round Top would expose his position to an attack from the rear and a possible sequential collapse of the federal defenses. Warren ordered Captain James Smith's Fourth New York Battery above the Devil's Den to fire a shell into a wooded area to the north of Round Top. Warren later described its effect:

> As the shot went whistling through the air the sound of it reached the enemy's troops and caused every one to look in the direction of it. This motion revealed to me the glistening of gun-barrels and bayonets of the enemy's line of battle, already formed and far outflanking the position of any of our troops; so that the line of his advance from his right to Little Round Top was unopposed. I have been particular in telling this, as the discovery was intensely thrilling to my feelings, and almost appalling.[73]

Warren sprang into action, hastening back down the slope to divert some troops of Sykes's V Corps to the top. He issued orders in the name of the commanding general. Two V Corps brigades answered his call—first, Colonel Strong Vincent's Third Brigade, First Division, followed by Brigadier General Stephen H. Weed's Third Brigade, Second Division. Warren personally helped to move up to the summit two guns belonging to First Lieutenant Charles E. Hazlett's Company D, Fifth U.S. Artillery.

While Union troops were scrambling to occupy Little Round Top, Brigadier General Evander M. Law's brigade and part of Brigadier General Jerome B. Robertson's brigade, both of Hood's division, struck the little hill with a terrible fury. Hood had ordered Law to launch a frontal attack in echelon across the Emmitsburg Road. Lee intended this attack in sequential waves to apply not only to brigades but also to divisions, starting on his right flank and gathering strength as it rolled up the Union army moving to the north. A preliminary exchange of artillery barrages altered Lee's plan.

Fragments from a Union shell ripped into General Hood's left arm while he was positioning his troops. The seriousness of his wound—he later lost the arm—removed him from the field of battle. While his comrades carried him away, as he recalled in his later years, he experienced "deep distress of mind and heart at the thought of the inevitable fate of my brave fellow-soldiers, who formed one of the grandest divisions of that world-renown army."[74] Command of that grand division devolved to Evander Law.

Contrary to Lee's grand design, when Law learned of the enemy's presence on Little Round Top, rather than risk exposing his right flank, he swept all the way across the western slope of Round Top and attacked its lesser neighbor from the south. Law's unauthorized change of direction interjected a strategy that had not formed a part of either army commander's battle plan.

A college professor in civilian life, Colonel Joshua Chamberlain led the 20th Maine Regiment in a bloody offensive that repelled a Confederate bid to take Little Round Top. For his victory, Chamberlain received the Medal of Honor.

Just as Colonel William C. Oates's Fifteenth Alabama Regiment (Law) started up the south slope of Little Round Top, the Confederates fell under intense fire. Oates called it "the most destructive fire I ever saw."[75] It came from Colonel Joshua L. Chamberlain's Twentieth Maine Regiment (Vincent). Chamberlain, a college professor in civilian life, arrived at the crest with 386 volunteers from Maine just in time to repulse the initial rebel thrust.

Thereafter, the Twentieth Maine withstood the attacks of the Alabamians and Texans of Law's brigade for two hours. (Although two brigades on each side participated in the battle, the action keyed on the Fifteenth Alabama and the Twentieth Maine because each formed the anchor of its respective army.) Vincent's orders to Chamberlain left nothing to question: "This is the left of the Union line. . . . You are to hold this ground at all costs."[76]

Law's orders to Oates were to take the high ground.

Several times during the battle, Chamberlain repositioned his regiment under heavy fire and fought off repeated whooping, firing Confederate attacks that threatened to overwhelm the men from Maine. Minutes before his Twentieth Maine ran out of ammunition, Chamberlain reached deep inside himself and seized upon the stuff of glory. Years later, he wrote of that moment:

> Five minutes more of such a defensive, and the last roll call would sound for us! Desperate as the chances were, there was nothing for it, but to take the offensive. I stepped to the colors. The men turned towards me. One word was enough,— "BAYONETS!"[77]

Chamberlain and his 200 men then charged "down into the face of half a thousand"[78] and overwhelmed Oates's attackers in savage, hand-to-hand fighting. Frail flesh succumbed to slashing steel and flashing blades in a wild killing foray. "The blood stood in puddles in some places on the rocks,"[79] Oates later recalled.

Chamberlain's charge netted several hundred prisoners. Scores of others on both sides died in the struggle, including Weed, O'Rorke, and Hazlett. And Vincent died later of wounds incurred during the struggle. Chamberlain received the Medal of Honor for his valorous performance on Little Round Top.

The stand on the little hill had proved costly to the federals, but—due in large measure to the quick actions of Gouverneur Warren and Joshua Chamberlain—they had held their flank. Chamberlain went on to occupy Round Top and further secure the Union left later that evening. Although much fighting still lay ahead, many military strategists believe that the federal stand on Little Round Top marked the turning point in the Battle of Gettysburg.

Chamberlain, reflecting on the battle 26 years later, recaptured the emotion of that experience: "The inspiration of a noble cause involving human interests wide and far, enables men to do things they did not dream themselves capable of before, and which they were not capable of alone. The consciousness of belonging, vitally, to something beyond individuality; of being part of a personality that reaches we know not where, in space and time, greatens the heart to the limit of the soul's ideal, and builds out the supreme of character."[80]

Union forces struggled to save the Federal's flag from Confederate capture. The three-day battle at Gettysburg yielded casualties in the tens of thousands and repelled the South's attempt to score a defining victory.

July 2: Blood and Fury along the Fishhook

The "supreme of character" was a common quality on both sides at Gettysburg on July 2, 1863. At 4:30 P.M., in a near-simultaneous action to the west of Little Round Top, Brigadier General Henry L. Benning's Georgia brigade and part of J. B. Robertson's brigade (both belonging to Hood/Law) swarmed into the Rose Woods and charged uphill into the Devil's Den, a rugged patch of rocks and boulders. They advanced into the guns of Captain Smith's Fourth New York Battery and Brigadier General J. H. Hobart Ward's Second Brigade. The Second Brigade formed a part of Major General David B. Birney's First Division. This action was the first of several to reveal the flawed deployment of Sickles's III Corps.

The III Corps comprised three divisions. Sickles ordered Birney's division to defend a three-quarter-mile stretch from Devil's Den in the south to the Peach Orchard to the north. Birney, in turn, assigned the defense of the woods on Houck's Ridge, just to the east of the Rose farm, plus the rock pile of Devil's Den, to Ward's Second Brigade. He further ordered Brigadier General Charles K. Graham's First Brigade to defend the salient at the Peach Orchard, and Colonel Regis de Trobriand's Third Brigade, the area in between.

Two regiments of Robertson's brigade spearheaded the Confederate attack. (His other two regiments had peeled off to attack Little Round Top.) But Robertson's orders were to take the Rose Woods and Devil's Den, and he intended to carry out his orders. Smith meant to stop him. His cannoneers fired furiously and nearly nonstop to stave off Robertson's advancing First Texas and Third Arkansas Regiments.

Smith's New Yorkers soon ran out of case shot—shells packed with iron or lead musket balls. "Give them shell!" Smith bellowed, "give them solid shot! Damn them, give them anything!"[81] His artillerists gave their all, but lost three Parrott guns—rifled cannons—in failing to stop the Confederates. Only a timely counterattack by Major James Cromwell's 124th New York Regiment (Ward) saved the federals from extinction.

Cromwell was killed instantly. Colonel Augustus Van Horne Ellis took command. He too was killed. But at this point the federals outnumbered the Confederates by two to one and finally succeeded in shoving back Robertson's over-matched regiments. The Union advantage soon faded in a blur of gray, when the 124th New York ran head-on into Benning's brigade, whose turn had come to join the battle. Benning had been slated to help take Little Round Top, but he diverted his brigade when he saw Robertson in dire difficulty and rushed to his aid. At the sight of the Georgians, someone shouted, "There is Benning; we are all right now."[82]

The rock formation called Devil's Den was the site of a bloody battle. Here a dead soldier lies where he fell, killed by enemy fire.

Spurring his Georgia boys onward, Benning whooped repeatedly in high rebel fashion, "Give them hell, boys, give them hell."[83] And they did. His Fifteenth and Twentieth Georgia Regiments joined with Robertson's regiments in driving Ward's bluecoats out of the Rose Woods. Benning's other two Georgia regiments—the Second and Seventeenth —attacked into Devil's Den and assailed the Fortieth New York (Ward) in a parallel action. Confusion and desperation reigned as the battle raged on, spilling over into a narrow gap between Devil's Den and the Round Tops. The gap soon became known as the Slaughter Pen for obvious reasons.

At 6:00 P.M., after two regiments of Law's brigade had joined the fighting from the south, Ward's forces finally yielded to the unrelenting Confederate attack. The Southerners moved in and planted their flag in the Devil's Den, where it remained for the rest of the battle at Gettysburg. James Bradford of the First Texas Regiment later called the battle at Devil's Den "one of the wildest, fiercest struggles of the war."[84] Like valor, wild, fierce struggles were commonplace at Gettysburg that day.

At 5:45 P.M., continuing Lee's plan of sequential attacks (in echelon), Brigadier General George T. Anderson's Georgia brigade (the last of Law's brigades) stepped off toward the Wheatfield, between the Rose Woods and the Peach Orchard salient. Anderson aimed his attack at the center of the line held by Colonel Regis de Trobriand's Third Brigade (Birney).

De Trobriand, who had sent two regiments to help out elsewhere, now faced Anderson's five regiments with only three of his own. The federals responded quickly to the developing danger, however, and reinforced de Trobriand with brigades under Colonels William S. Tilton (First) and Jacob B. Sweitzer (Second) of Brigadier General James Barnes's First Division, V Corps (Sykes), along with two regiments from Brigadier General Andrew A. Humphreys's Second Division, III Corps.

With the advantage of numerical strength and more favorable positioning, these troops repulsed Anderson's attack. Charge upon countercharge followed until Anderson, recognizing his lack of progress, delayed any further action pending the arrival of fresh Confederate troops. These arrived in the body of Major General Lafayette McLaws's First Brigade, commanded by Brigadier General Joseph B. Kershaw.

Tilton recognized the new threat at once and adjusted his brigade's alignment to meet it. In so doing, however, he

exposed Sweitzer's flank. As a result, division commander Barnes, apparently unnerved, pulled back both brigades. Only de Trobriand's small band remained to halt the advance of two Confederate brigades. De Trobriand called for help. Major General Winfield S. Hancock, II Corps commander, heeded his call, ordering Brigadier General John C. Caldwell's First Division to leave its position on Cemetery Ridge and lend a much-needed hand to de Trobriand.

With de Trobriand's depleted brigade under attack from all sides except the rear, Caldwell obliged. He came under attack almost immediately but his three brigades succeeded in driving the Confederates back across the Wheatfield and through the Rose Woods. His success was short-lived. Kershaw's call for help brought Brigadier General Paul J. Semmes's brigade (McLaws) rushing onto the field. Caldwell's troops cut down many of them, including Semmes, who fell mortally wounded. But the battle soon turned in favor of the Confederates.

Brigadier General William T. Wofford's brigade now advanced quietly toward the Wheatfield and struck Caldwell's right (north) flank, in concert with Kershaw, Semmes, and Anderson, who attacked Caldwell's center and left flank. With his division threatened with total destruction, Caldwell withdrew to a ridge behind Plum Run. Sweitzer's brigade then rejoined the fray and engaged their enemies in brutal hand-to-hand fighting. A Union lieutenant observing the action from Little Round Top, exclaimed, "What a hell is there down there in that valley!"[85]

At 6:15 P.M., the hell moved northward into the Peach Orchard. Kershaw's South Carolina brigade started another bloodbath with an attack on Stony Hill, set between the Wheatfield and the Peach Orchard. Thirty cannons of III Corps and the Artillery Reserve decimated the ranks of

the Carolinians. McLaw then threw in his two left-flank brigades, commanded by Brigadier Generals William Barksdale and William T. Wofford.

Barksdale, a tall, silver-maned Mississippian, had pestered McLaw all afternoon for permission to attack. "General, let me go," he had repeatedly implored. "General, let me charge."[86] McLaw finally gave him the nod and Barksdale led from out in front of the whole line—some say on foot; others say mounted on his charger. Either way, the irrepressible commander led his brigade in a headlong charge toward the Peach Orchard and Sickles's III Corps defenders. Wofford followed.

One Confederate lieutenant afterward described Barksdale's wildly determined assault as "the most magnificent charge I witnessed during the war," while a Union colonel viewed it from a different perspective in a similar fashion as "the grandest charge that was ever made by mortal man."[87]

Crashing with cavalier abandon through the stout rail fences lining both sides of the Emmitsburg Road, Barksdale's Mississippians advanced on the run, firing as they ran, just north of the Peach Orchard. Two regiments of Pennsylvanians—the Fifth-Seventh and 114th of Brigadier General Charles K. Graham's First Brigade (Birney)—rushed forth to meet them at the Sherfy House. A bloody clash ensued. Both sides suffered great losses. Graham's forces could not withstand the rebel onslaught and pulled back into the Peach Orchard.

Graham tried to regroup his brigade and continue the fight, but his losses mounted dramatically in a short fight there. The 141st Pennsylvania lost 149 men of its original complement of 200. Graham fell wounded and was captured. Barksdale's Mississippians quickly corralled almost 1,000 of his men and sent Graham and his First Brigaders to the rear. But Barksdale wasn't done yet.

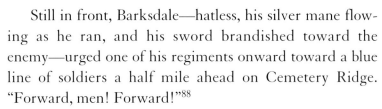

Still in front, Barksdale—hatless, his silver mane flowing as he ran, and his sword brandished toward the enemy—urged one of his regiments onward toward a blue line of soldiers a half mile ahead on Cemetery Ridge. "Forward, men! Forward!"[88]

And so they rushed—straight into the mouths of 40 Union cannon, specially assembled to stop them. Not a man among them reached the distant ridge lined with blue.

The fierce Union cannonading forced the Mississippians to fall back westward and reform along Plum Run. They left half their number dead or wounded on the battlefield, including their commander. That evening, scouts from a Vermont regiment found the wounded Barksdale and brought him into their lines. He had been shot through both legs and the chest. Barksdale paid the price that glory all too often requires. He died before daybreak.

In the meantime, when Wofford attacked into the Peach Orchard, he caught the Second New Hampshire Regiment (Second Division, Third Brigade, III Corps) facing south and firing into Kershaw's brigade. When Second Division commander Brigadier General Andrew A. Humphreys realized their exposed position, he ordered them to retreat. But not before the New Hampshire regiment suffered enormous casualties—21 of 24 officers and nearly half of its men.

As the fighting moved northward, Barksdale's regrouped Mississippians attacked the left flank of Humphreys's two northernmost brigades. Simultaneously, Major General Richard H. Anderson, one of A. P. Hill's division commanders, ordered the brigades of Brigadier General Cadmus M. Wilcox and Colonel David Lang to attack their center. At this point, III Corps commander Sickles took a hit from a rebel cannonball. Meade asked Hancock to take over III Corps and to reinforce Humphreys.

Hancock found Brigadier General William Harrow's First Minnesota Regiment (First Brigade, Second Division) nearby and charged them with the task of checking Anderson's advance. The Minnesotans held off the rebel brigades but paid dearly, losing 82 percent of its 262-man contingent. Humphreys's embattled Second Division (III Corps) lost 1,500 of its original complement of 4,000 men.

In one final effort to hold the Wheatfield, Brigadier General Romeyn B. Ayres's Second Division, V Corps—consisting of mostly U.S. Regulars—joined the battle. Two Regular brigades under Colonels Hannibal Day and Sidney Burbank fought with a singular fury but succeeded only in adding torrents of blood to a field already drenched with it. Captain Richard Robbins of the Eleventh U.S. Infantry (Burbank) recalled: "The few hundred yards to the foot of Little Round Top, already strewn with our disabled comrades, became a very charnel house, and every step was marked by ghastly lines of dead and wounded."[89] They called "the few hundred yards" the Valley of Death. In less than an hour, the two Regular brigades lost 829 men killed, wounded, or missing—or a loss rate of almost one-third of the 2,613 men engaged.

Three brigade commanders were killed in the frenzied action, and Sickles lost his right leg to a cannon ball. Regiment fought regiment as the bloody conflict seesawed this way and that until dark. At its end, the Confederates had succeeded in forcing the federals out of the Wheatfield and back to Cemetery Ridge—where Sickles should have been in the first place.

By the time shadows began lengthening across the Pennsylvania countryside, the Confederates, despite their failure to dislodge the federals from Little Round Top, could claim a solid edge in the day's fighting. They had rolled back Meade's defenses in three places—at the Devil's Den, the Wheatfield, and the Peach Orchard. And in the

Union General Daniel Sickles (seated) and his staff, after the battle of Gettysburg, in which Sickles lost his right leg to a cannonball.

prolonged daylight of a new summer much time remained to prosecute Lee's echeloned attack to the north before darkness would intervene in the fighting.

About 6:30 P.M., Anderson sent a third brigade—Brigadier General Ambrose R. Wright's—to attack Cemetery Ridge to the north of Wilcox and Lang. Wright somehow found a gap in the Union defenses and drove all the way to the foot of Cemetery Ridge. But when Wilcox and Lang retired in the face of fierce resistance from the First Minnesota, and when relief from Anderson's two uncommitted brigades failed to materialize, Wright relinquished his foothold at the base of the ridge and joined Wilcox and Lang in retirement. When dusk turned to darkness, the federal defense line along Cemetery Ridge remained in tact.

Darkness did not end the fighting, however, as to the north and east of the federal lines, Lieutenant General Richard S. Ewell's Second Army Corps had yet to play out its role in Lee's master plan. Although his artillery had commenced shelling Cemetery and Culp's Hills when Longstreet began his attack at 4:00 P.M., an overwhelming presence of Union artillery on both hills soon silenced the rebel guns. Far from striking in concert with Longstreet, Ewell failed to launch his diversionary attack until the fighting along the fishhook's shank had essentially ceased.

Finally, at 7:00 P.M., Ewell sent Early's division against Cemetery Hill, but Union defenders repulsed his badly coordinated attack. Moreover, Ewell's delay in launching his attack had enabled Meade to focus his full attention on Longstreet.

At 8:00 P.M., Ewell launched a much-belated attack on the twin peaks of Culp's Hill. Geary's Second Division of Slocum's XII Corps held the north peak in entrenched positions. Major General Edward Johnson's division (Ewell) assaulted the south peak and established a foothold near the base of it. But Johnson came under heavy fire from David McM. Gregg's horse artillery, positioned farther south, and could advance no farther. The second day's fighting ended. Both sides lost another 9,000 men.

Lee's army had gained more ground, but Meade's army remained entrenched in its strong position. Overall, the Army of Northern Virginia had performed poorly over the day, lacking coordination and failing to exploit its successes. So, who bore responsibility for the Confederates' lackluster showing? "The fault was at the top," avers John M. Taylor, one of Lee's biographers. "Of Lee's three corps commanders, Longstreet was disgruntled, Ewell was inept, and Hill was unwell. Lee himself seemed much less disposed to assert control than at Antietam and Chancellorsville."[90]

Hill had taken ill the day before and evidence suggests that Lee himself might have been experiencing a stomach distress of some sort. Whatever the cause, the effect was sufficient (as Taylor points out) for Douglas S. Freeman to write that on July 2 "the Army of Northern Virginia was without a commander."[91]

That night, while the great battle's outcome remained at issue, Jeb Stuart and his three brigades of cavalry cantered into the Confederate camp. Lee greeted his cavalryman curtly: "Well, General Stuart, you are here at last."[92] He spoke not another word. Some say that coming from Lee these eight words represented a severe rebuke, and perhaps they did. But it seems likely that Stuart's arrival—however tardy—could only augur well and offer renewed hope in Lee's mind for a decisive Confederate victory on the morrow.

July 3: Pickett's Charge, Stuart's Sally, and Battle's End

Lee's strategy on July 3, 1863 was to attack Meade's forces where they stood with a massive thrust at their center. Led by Confederate General George Pickett, the now-famous "Pickett's Charge" became a bloody defeat due to ceaseless Union artillery fire.

O n the night of July 2, both army commanders held councils of war. Meade met with his corps commanders at the Leister house, seeking their views on the day's fighting and on prospects for the morrow. After a discussion period, Major General Daniel Butterfield, Meade's chief of staff, posed the crucial question: Should the army remain in place and fight it out, or should it slip away in the night to a stronger defensive line to the south, perhaps along Big Pipe Creek? A consensus voted to stay. "Such then is the decision,"[93] Meade said softly and adjourned the meeting.

Before John Gibbon left the meeting, Meade spoke privately to him. "Gibbon, if Lee attacks me tomorrow it will be on *your front,*"[94] he predicted. Gibbon's Second Division, II Corps, occupied the center of the Union line on Cemetery Ridge. Gibbons welcomed the challenge. Later that night, when Meade learned of the rebel foothold on the lower peak of Culp's Hill, he authorized Henry Slocum's XII Corps to retake its lost territory at daybreak. If Lee attacked, he would find Meade ready for him.

Meanwhile, in the Confederate camp across the vale on Seminary Ridge, Lee also met with his corps commanders to critique the day's battles and why the Confederate attacks had faltered at the crucial moments. "The whole affair was disjointed," groused Major Walter H. Taylor of Lee's staff. "There was an utter absence of accord in the movements of the several commands, and no decisive results attended the operations of the second day."[95] Despite a virtual stalemate after two days of fighting, Lee still saw the opportunity for a decisive victory.

In his report, Lee noted: "The result of the day's operations induced the belief that, with proper concert of attack, and with the increased support that the positions gained on the right would enable the artillery to render the assaulting columns, we should ultimately succeed, and it was accordingly determined to continue the attack."[96] Lee's grand strategy remained unchanged—attack Meade where he stood.

Lee's initial plan for July 3 probably called for a full-scale, *coordinated* attack all along the line in the west, while Ewell assaulted Culp's Hill in the east. At the same time, at least in theory, Stuart's cavalry would swing around Gettysburg and Ewell's corps and prepare to assail the Union positions from the rear, following an anticipated Confederate breakthrough. But that did not happen.

At daybreak on July 3, 26 Union guns unleashed a skull-thumping barrage from various XII Corps (Slocum) positions on the upper (north) peak of Culp's Hill. Major General Edward Johnson's Confederates on the south

Rebel troops, who had taken up a stronghold at the base of Culp's Hill were met by Henry Slocom's 12th Corps in a bloody attempt to retake the territory. Union artillery fire forced the Confederates to choose— either attack or die.

peak hunkered down. "The whole hillside seemed enveloped in a blaze," recalled Major William W. Goldsborough, commander of the First Maryland Battalion of Brigadier General George H. Steuart's brigade, "and the balls could be heard to strike the breastworks [temporary fortifications] like hailstones upon the roof tops."[97] The Union fire forced the rebels to attack or die.

When the bombardment lifted, three of Johnson's brigades rushed the Union-held peak, shouting their customary rebel yells, which drew the attention of Union riflemen above. According to Lieutenant Colonel David Zabel, commander of the Fourteenth Louisiana Regiment of Colonel Jesse M. Williams's brigade, their shrieks served "no other purpose but to intensify a more galling fire in our front."[98] Anderson's rebels attacked repeatedly; Slocum's Yankees matched attack with counterattack. The fighting flared for seven hours.

At 11:00 A.M., Anderson finally quit trying to take the hill. In his report, he noted: "The enemy were too securely entrenched and in too great numbers to be dislodged by the force at my command." In conclusion, he averred, "All had been done that it was possible to do."[99] The federal defenders had sustained 1,082 casualties; the Confederates, about twice as many. Moreover, Lee could no longer count on help from Ewell's fought-out corps in the fighting still to come that afternoon.

Lee had intended Ewell (Johnson) to coordinate his attack against Culp's Hill with Longstreet's renewed attack on the Union left. But any hope for a coordinated attack fell by the wayside when Slocum's guns set Johnson's division in motion at dawn. Lee revised his attack plan. Rather than mount a concerted attack along the fishhook, he decided to gang his forces together for a massive assault against the center of Meade's line (Gibbon) on Cemetery Ridge. This plan incorporated the military principle of *mass,* a concentration of force at the decisive time and place.

Lee met with Longstreet early on July 3 and outlined his new plan: Pickett's fresh division (Longstreet) up from Chambersburg would spearhead the attack; Heth's and Pender's divisions (Hill) would support Pickett; Longstreet would command. Stuart, in the meantime, was to range behind Ewell's corps and—in concert with Longstreet's attack—strike Cemetery Ridge from the rear. Again,

Longstreet disagreed with Lee's thinking, still preferring to coax Meade into the attack by feinting at his right. "No," Lee insisted again, "I am going to take them where they are."[100]

Longstreet estimated the size of his proposed attack force at about 15,000 men and said: "I have been a soldier, I may say, from the ranks up to the position I now hold. I have been in pretty much all kinds of skirmishes . . . and I think I can safely say there never was a body of fifteen thousand men who could make that attack success-fully."[101] His evaluation fell on unreceptive ears. Lee had made up his mind.

At 1:00 P.M., Colonel Edward P. Alexander, Longstreet's artillery officer, threw up his arm and thrust it forward. One gun fired in response, then a second—a prearranged signal—then 140 Confederate cannon spoke as one and the earth shook for miles untold. Captain Charles E. Raines observed the fire of his Virginia battery on the artillery positions of Howard's XI Corps. "It was admirable shooting," he recalled. "They raked the whole line of batteries, killed and wounded the men and horses, and blew up the caissons [two-wheeled ammunition carriers] rapidly. I saw one shell go through six horses standing broadside."[102] Alexander's barrage—the largest ever witnessed on the North American continent up till then—lasted for two hours.

While the bombardment was softening Union defenses for Pickett's assault, Stuart and his three brigades of cavalry proceeded around the federals' right to a location about five miles east of Gettysburg, along and north of Hanover Road. At about 2:30 P.M., he occupied an elevated wooded region known as Cress's Ridge and positioned his brigades for a run at Meade's rear. But Meade had anticipated just such a move. To counter Stuart, he had dispatched the First and Third Brigades of Brigadier General David McM. Gregg's

Second Division, Cavalry Corps, plus the Third Division's Second Brigade, commanded by the newly promoted Brigadier General George Armstrong Custer.

Gregg realized that a rematch of Brandy Station was in the making and sent out a line of dismounted blue skirmishers. Stuart answered in kind, and the cavalrymen clashed at long range and on foot. After several hours of indecisively exchanging small-arms fire at a distance, Stuart sallied forth from Cress's Ridge to brush aside the federal horsemen.

On the far side of Cemetery Ridge, the Confederate artillery barrage lifted at 2:00 P.M., and artillery chief Alexander told Longstreet, "Our only chance is to follow it up now, to strike while the iron is hot."[103] Longstreet, still adamantly opposed to the scheme, reluctantly instructed Major General George E. Pickett to carry out Lee's orders. And the futile clash of men and arms that history has come to know as "Pickett's Charge" began.

At about 2:15 P.M., some 13,500 gray-clad attackers emerged from the woods opposite Cemetery Ridge and west of Emmitsburg Road where they had formed. They immediately came under heavy fire from the guns of Brigadier General Henry Jackson Hunt, Meade's chief artillerist, who had earlier withheld his fire to conserve ammunition. Even so, the "Johnny Rebs" advanced steadily toward a copse of trees at the Union center that Alexander's guns had focused on. They walked, then trotted, then ran, crouched, with flags waving and rebel yells piercing the air.

Many Union soldiers took shelter behind a low stone wall in front of the ridge. A hundred yards north of the copse, the wall took a 90-degree turn—forever known as "The Angle"—and ran eastward for 80 yards before turning northward again. Men of the Seventy-First Pennsylvania (part of Gibbon's division) looked on with wonder and horror at thousands of onrushing rebels belonging to the brigades of Brigadier Generals Lewis A. Armistead and Richard B. Garnett (Pickett). One eyewitness later wrote:

> Men fire into each other's faces. There are bayonet-thrusts, sabre-strokes, pistol shots; . . . men . . . spinning around like tops, throwing out their arms, gulping up blood, falling, legless, armless, headless . . . ghastly heaps of dead men.[104]

First one Yankee broke and fled, then another and another, until finally the entire Seventy-First Pennsylvania cut and ran. Armistead surely expected the rest of the Union line to follow the lead of the Seventy-First and crumble. He must have felt total victory within his grasp when he ran to the front of his brigade and led it in pursuit of the Pennsylvanians. Raising his hat on the point of his sword, he shouted, "Come forward, Virginians! Come on, Boys, we must give them the cold steel; who will follow me?"[105] Armistead leaped over the low wall and charged toward the battery of Lieutenant Alonzo Cushing (II Corps).

Cushing, already mortally wounded, yelled to his brigade commander: "Webb, I will give them one more shot!"[106] He pulled his cannon's lanyard and unleashed a hail of case shot into the face of the attackers, then fell dead beside his guns. Moments later, three bullets from the Seventy-Second Pennsylvania to the left of Cushing's guns, struck Armistead and he fell dead only a few feet from Cushing.

To the left of Armistead's Virginians, Heth's division, now under Pettigrew's command, advanced into the Angle—some say the Bloody Angle—and experienced a similar blood-letting. Once inside the fences along Emmitsburg Road, Pettigrew's men fell under a raking artillery fire. One observer wrote later that the Confederates "were at once enveloped in a dense cloud of dust. Arms, heads, blankets, guns, and knapsacks were tossed into the clear air. A moan went up from the field distinctly to be heard among the storm of battle."[107] Miraculously, Pettigrew's division and two brigades of North Carolinians under Major General Isaac R. Trimble advanced as far as the stone wall north of the Angle. But federal reinforcements arrived to stem the Confederate tide and it receded from what the Union soon came to call the High Water Mark of the rebellion.

Sadly, for the Confederate cause, fully five of their brigades in position to cover Pettigrew's left and to attack stood by and did nothing—except to watch the slaughter of their comrades. The storm of exploding metal had stripped the attackers of many of their leaders. Without leaders, Pickett's Charge petered out. Pickett, watching from the Codori farm, turned his horse's head toward Seminary Ridge. The charge was over.

Lee's grand plan had failed. After the charge, Lee accepted responsibility for its failure and asked Pickett to reassemble his division for a counterattack. Pickett bowed his head and replied, "General Lee, I have no division now."[108]

Pickett never forgave Lee for the destruction of his fine division, which had taken barely more than an hour. Among its participants, the charge claimed casualties totaling nearly 66 percent. Union losses tallied about 25 percent. But there was some fighting still to be done. While Pickett's battle was ending, Stuart's fray was flaring hotly.

Two of Stuart's brigades attacked the federals with sabers flashing under a hot afternoon sun. Custer's Second Brigade of Michiganders advanced to meet them. Colonel John R. Chambliss's sword-swinging rebels repulsed Custer's Fifth Michigan. But Custer quickly rallied his brand-new Seventh Michigan. Drawing his sword and shouting, "Come on, you Wolverines!"[109] he led them across open ground straight toward the Rummel Farm.

Custer's attackers carried themselves "in splendid style"[110] until they ran into the First Virginia, of Brigadier General Fitzhugh Lee's brigade, sheltered behind a fence. Some of the Michiganders dismounted and began tearing down the fence to allow their comrades to break through and assault the Virginians from the rear. Colonel William D. Mann urged the bluecoats on: "Kill all you can and do your best for each other."[111] Their best fell short of their aims and the attack faltered.

Private Allan Price, an onlooker from the Sixth Michigan, later reported, "The 7th Michigan made a charge and got all cut to pieces. It was the first charge they ever made and it was awful work."[112] The Confederates pressed their advantage and surged forward.

Brigade commander Wade Hampton, looking on from Cress's Ridge, feared that the Confederate regiments were advancing too far, but their movement was too rapid to recall by messenger. Hampton grabbed his personal colors and spurred his warhorse Butler down the ridge toward his endangered horsemen, shouting for them to fall back. Hampton's adjutant, Major T. J. Barker, mistook his commander's action for a signal to attack. Barker rounded up the rest of Hampton's regiments and charged after the surprised commander. Gregg countered their advance with Custer.

Custer rode over to Colonel Charles H. Town, commander of his First Michigan Cavalry, and said, "General Gregg directs us to put those people out of action. Are you agreeable?"[113] He was indeed.

"By all means, General!"[114] he said, and Custer's Wolverines wheeled out of the trees by column of squadrons, crossed Low Dutch Road, and rode out into the open field to meet Hampton's brigade of Carolinians and Georgians.

At a trot, in front by four lengths, Custer yelled, "Keep

The house of Abraham Bryan, an African-American, stood only yards from the crest of Cemetery Ridge, where Union forces held their line against waves of Confederate attack.

to your sabers, boys! Keep to your sabers!" As they neared Hampton's rebels, Custer rose to a gallop. With his ringlets and saber waving in the air, he again shrieked, "Come on, you Wolverines!"[115] And 5,000 horsemen collided at a combined speed of 50 miles an hour.

Captain William E. Miller of the Third Pennsylvania, who would later receive the Medal of Honor for his part in the action, described the clash afterward: "The meeting was as the crash of ocean waves breaking upon a rock-bound coast, and men and horses rolled and tossed like foam upon its crest."[116]

In the clash of cavaliers, Custer fell from his horse, but shook it off, mounted a riderless steed, and fought on. Hampton took a saber slash to the head and retaliated with a stroke of his own. Several Wolverines encircled him, seeking retribution. Sergeant Nat Price of the First North Carolina dashed to Hampton's aid. "General, General, they are too many for us," he cried. "For God's sake, leap your horse over the fence; I'll die before they have you!"[117] Despite his flowing wound, Hampton, with Price's help, fled to safety.

The cavalry battle lasted for three hours—long after Pickett's Charge had ended—with neither side dominating. Stuart called off his horsemen at dusk and returned to Lee's army. Gregg's forces remained in possession of the battlefield. The federals reported 286 casualties; the Confederates, 181. Both sides claimed a victory that neither side had won.

The Battle of Gettyburg ended with the daylight on the third day of fighting.

What They Did There: Americans Will Never Forget

As Lee and the Army of Northern Virginia were forced to retreat across the Potomac, Meade's Union forces were slow to pursue—a fact that angered President Lincoln.

On July 4, 1863, General Meade braced his forces for another Confederate attack, while General Lee prepared his troops for a federal counterattack. Neither occurred. Each side spent the day watching the other across the open fields. As they watched, a hard, driving rain started falling, as if to wash away the blood and obscenities of three days of fighting.

Meade's Army of the Potomac sustained losses in excess of 3,155 dead, 14,529 wounded, and 5,365 missing—a total of 23,049, roughly a quarter of its original force. Lee's Army of Northern Virginia recorded losses of more than 2,500 dead, almost 13,000 wounded, and some 5,500 missing—a sum of 21,000, about a third of its total force at the start of hostilities. Some chroniclers believe that postbattle deaths and desertions elevated Confederate losses to about 28,000 casualties. Lee accepted full blame for his losses.

Brigadier General John D. Imboden, one of Lee's cavalry commanders, later wrote of a conversation he had shared with Lee on the night of July 3, in which Lee said:

> "I never saw troops behave more magnificently than Pickett's division of Virginians did today in that grand charge against the enemy. And if they had been supported as they were to have been—but, for some reason not fully explained to me, were not— we would have held the position and the day would have been ours." After a moment's pause he added in a loud voice, in a tone almost of agony, "Too bad! *Too bad! OH TOO BAD!*"[118]

Lee began his withdrawal on the night of July 4. At 5:30 P.M., he sent Imboden's cavalry southward the way they had come to guard the Confederate wagon train and screen the mountain passes. Well past dark, Lee's infantry headed west out the Fairfield Road, with Hill's corps leading the way, Longstreet's following, and Ewell's acting as the rear guard. Meade made no effort to pursue them until July 5, much to President Lincoln's consternation. "We had them within our grasp," he lamented. "We had only to stretch forth our hands and they were ours."[119] Lincoln's frustration was understandable.

While Lee was preparing to withdraw from Gettysburg on July 4, General John C. Pemberton was surrendering Vicksburg, Mississippi, to Union commander General Ulysses S. Grant, which effectively split the Confederacy in half. As Lincoln put it, "The Father of Waters once more flows unvexed to the sea."[120] The capitulation of the last Confederate port on the Mississippi in the West (now the midwest), combined with Meade's total destruction of Lee's army in the North, might have ended the war.

Instead, Meade and his mangled army pursued Lee's decimated ranks only with great caution. Had Meade elected to pursue Lee promptly and to attack him with vigor, his army might have caught and destroyed Lee's army at the Potomac River, which had risen under the driving rain to form a natural barrier. Meade might have used the swollen river as an anvil upon which to hammer the Army of Northern Virginia. Meade's failure to do so unduly limited his victory and enabled Lee to complete a successful withdrawal to Virginia on July 13. Hence the war dragged on for another year and 10 months.

On the other hand, had Lee defeated Meade in their chance encounter outside the small Pennsylvania town—which he came very close to doing—Lee would have likely added to his growing myth of invincibility. Northerners, already wearying of a war with no end in sight, might have pressured their government into suing for peace. Any accord between the Union and the Confederacy most probably would have seen the preservation of slavery, or the permanent diminution of the United States of America, or both. How these eventualities might have affected American westward expansion, the longevity of slavery, future relations between the U.S.A. and the C.S.A., and the role of Americans in the world theater can only be imagined. The possibilities are infinite—and not necessarily pleasant from the perspective of today's Americans.

Many aficionados and practitioners of the military arts point to the Union victory at Vicksburg as the turning point in the Civil War and with good reason. But that does not detract from the huge significance of the Battle of Gettysburg, which historians generally regard as the High Tide of the Confederacy. Lee's defeat cost the Confederacy far more in lost manpower than either Lee or the limited

President Lincoln (hatless at center) addresses the crowd at the Gettysburg Cemetery Memorial, November 19, 1863, forever after to be known as the Gettysburg Address.

resources of the South could sustain. After Gettysburg, Lee was never again able to mount a major offensive. His defeat marked the beginning of the end for the South. The Confederate tide began to ebb and receded all the way to Appomattox Court House, Virginia—the scene of Lee's last defeat.

In this sense, it can be strongly argued that the Battle of Gettysburg marks the true turning point in the War Between the States. What cannot be argued is the gratitude felt by successive generations of Americans for those who fought at Gettysburg and for what they did there. President Lincoln's words of November 19, 1863, spoken in the dedication ceremonies of the national cemetery now adjoining Cemetery Hill, still speak to the ages: "The world will little note, nor long remember what we say here, but it can never forget what they did here."[121] Americans will never forget.

1860

November 6   Abraham Lincoln elected president of the United States

December 20   South Carolina secedes from the Union, followed by Mississippi, Florida, Alabama, Georgia, Louisiana, and Texas over the next six weeks

1861

February 8   Seceding states form a federation called the Confederate States of America

March 4   Lincoln takes the oath of office

April 12   Confederate gun batteries open fire on Fort Sumter, South Carolina; the Civil War (or the War Between the States) begins

April 17   Virginia secedes from the Union, followed quickly by Arkansas, Tennessee, and North Carolina

December 20
South Carolina secedes from the Union, followed by Mississippi, Florida, Alabama, Georgia, Louisiana, and Texas over the next six weeks

February 8
Seceding states form a federation called the Confederate States of America

April 12
Confederate gun batteries open fire on Fort Sumter, South Carolina; the Civil War (or the War Between the States) begins

November 6
Abraham Lincoln elected President of the United States

1860

1861

April 17
Virginia secedes from the Union, followed quickly by Arkansas, Tennessee, and North Carolina

Timeline

April 18	Lincoln orders blockade of ports from South Carolina to Texas; Virginia and North Carolina added eight days later
August 10	Battle of Wilson's Creek; Confederates defeat Brigadier General Nathaniel S. Lyon's forces; Lyon is killed

1862

February 6	General Ulysses S. Grant launches Union campaign in the West (now midwest); seizes Fort Henry on the Tennessee River
February 16	Grant seizes Fort Donelson on the Cumberland River
April 4	General George B. McClellan launches Peninsula Campaign
April 6-7	Battle of Shiloh (Pittsburg Landing); Grant's army mauled in a bloody but inconclusive battle; Confederate General A. S. Johnston is killed
April 24	Union Commodore David G. Farragut captures New Orleans

April 6-7
Battle of Shiloh (Pittsburg Landing); Grant's army mauled in a bloody but inconclusive battle; Confederate General A. S. Johnston is killed

April 4
General George B. McClellan launches Peninsula Campaign

August 29-30
Second Battle of Bull Run (Second Manassas); Lee ousts Brigadier General John Pope's newly formed (Union) Army of Virginia from Virginia

January 1
President Lincoln signs Emancipation Proclamation

July 4-13
Lee withdraws to Virginia; Meade follows cautiously

July 1-3
Battle of Gettysburg; Major General George G. Meade's Army of the Potomac prevails over General Robert E. Lee's Army of Northern Virginia in limited victory

1862   **1863**

June 25-July1
Lee defeats McClellan in Seven Days' Battles; Peninsula Campaign fails

September 17
Battle of Antietam (Sharpsburg); Lee and McClellan fight to a standoff

May 1-5
Battle of Chancellorsville; General Robert E. Lee's Army of Northern Virginia defeats Major General Joseph ("Fighting Joe") Hooker's Army of the Potomac

June 9
Battle of Brandy Station; the largest cavalry battle of the war between the forces of Confederate commander Major General James Ewell Brown "Jeb" Stuart Union commander Major General Alfred Pleasonton

June 25-July 1   Lee defeats McClellan in Seven Days' Battles; Peninsula Campaign fails

August 29-30   Second Battle of Bull Run (Second Manassas); Lee ousts Brigadier General John Pope's newly formed (Union) Army of Virginia from Virginia

September 17   Battle of Antietam (Sharpsburg); Lee and McClellan fight to a standoff

September 22   President Lincoln issues preliminary document outlining plans for emancipating runaway slaves

1863

January 1   President Lincoln signs Emancipation Proclamation

May 1-5   Battle of Chancellorsville; General Robert E. Lee's Army of Northern Virginia defeats Major General Joseph "Fighting Joe" Hooker's Army of the Potomac

May 10   Brigadier General Thomas J. "Stonewall" Jackson dies of wounds received at Chancellorsville

June 9   Battle of Brandy Station; the largest cavalry battle of the war between the forces of Confederate commander Major General James Ewell Brown "Jeb" Stuart Union commander Major General Alfred Pleasonton

July 1-3   Battle of Gettysburg; Major General George G. Meade's Army of the Potomac prevails over General Robert E. Lee's Army of Northern Virginia in limited victory

July 4-13   Lee withdraws to Virginia; Meade follows cautiously

July 4   Vicksburg, Mississippi, surrenders to Grant

CHAPTER 1

1. Quoted in Jeffry D. Wert, *Custer: The Controversial Life of George Armstrong Custer*. New York: Simon & Schuster, 1996, p. 77.
2. Quoted in D. A. Kinsley, *Custer: Favor the Bold, A Soldier's Story*. New York: Promontory Press, 1992, pp. 120-21.
3. Ibid., p. 121.
4. Douglas Southall Freeman, *Lee's Lieutenants: A Study in Command*. Vol. 1 *Manassas to Malvern Hill*. New York: Charles Scribner's Sons, 1942, p. 283.
5. Shelby Foote and the Editors of Time-Life, *The Civil War: A Narrative*. Vol. 7, Gettysburg to Draft Riots, 40th Anniversary Edition. Alexandria, VA: Time-Life Books, 1999, p. 21.
6. Quoted in ibid.
7. Quoted in Wert, *Custer*, p. 78.
8. Ibid., p. 77.
9. Ibid., p. 78.
10. Quoted in Rush's Lancers, "The Sixth Pennsylvania Cavalry at the Battle of Brandy Station, June 9, 1863," 2000. *www.rushslancers.com/brandy/html*.
11. Ibid.
12. Foote and the Editors of Time-Life, *The Civil War*, p. 23.
13. Quoted in Kinsley, *Custer*, p. 123.
14. Quoted in Foote and the Editors of Time-Life, *The Civil War*, p. 23.
15. Quoted in Kinsley, *Custer*, p. 125.
16. Ibid.

CHAPTER 2

17. Quoted in Charles F. Romanus, "The Civil War, 1861," in *American Military History*. Vol. 1, 1775-1902. Edited by Maurice Matloff. Conshohocken, PA: Combined Books, 1996, p. 184.
18. Quoted in Nancy A. Colbert, *The Firing on Fort Sumter: A Splintered Nation Goes to War*. Greensboro, NC: Morgan Reynolds, 2001, p. 62.
19. Ibid., p. 78.
20. Quoted in Gail B. Stewart, *Weapons of War: The Civil War*. American War Library. San Diego, CA: Lucent Books, 2000, p. 8.
21. Ibid., p. 9.
22. Quoted in Gerald S. Henig and Eric Niderost, *Civil War Firsts: The Legacies of America's Bloodiest Conflict*. Mechanicsburg, PA: Stackpole Books, 2001, p. 38.
23. Henig and Niderost, *Civil War Firsts*, p. 38.
24. Quoted in Mark E. Neely, Jr., *The Abraham Lincoln Encyclopedia*. New York: Da Capo Press, 1982, p. 32.

25. Quoted in Fletcher Pratt, *A Short History of the Civil War: Ordeal by Fire*. Mineola, NY: Dover Publications, 1997, p. 11.
26. Quoted in Bruce Catton, *The Civil War*. The American Heritage Library. New York: American Heritage Press, 1985, p. 41.
27. Quoted in Neely, *The Abraham Lincoln Encyclopedia*, p. 199.
28. Quoted in Catton, *The Civil War*, p. 58.
29. Quoted in Neely, *The Abraham Lincoln Encyclopedia*, p. 104.
30. Quoted in Catherine Clinton, *Scholastic Encyclopedia of the Civil War*. New York: Scholastic, 1999, p. 62.
31. Ibid., p. 63.

CHAPTER 3

32. Quoted in David Eggenberger, *An Encyclopedia of Battles: Accounts of Over 1,560 Battles from 1479 B.C. to the Present*. Mineola, NY: Dover Publications, 1985, p. 21.
33. Quoted in Craig L. Symonds, *Gettysburg: A Battlefield Atlas*. Baltimore, MD: Nautical & Aviation Publishing, 1999, p. 15.
34. Ibid.
35. Quoted in Foote and the Editors of Time-Life, *The Civil War*, p. 34.
36. Ibid., p. 35.
37. Quoted in Pratt, *A Short History of the Civil War*. pp. 204, 206.
38. Ibid., p. 206.
39. Ibid., p. 207.
40. Quoted in Foote and the Editors of Time-Life, *The Civil War*, p. 38.
41. Ibid., p. 39.
42. Quoted in Mark Grimsley and Brooks D. Simpson, *Gettysburg: A Battlefield Guide*. Lincoln, NE: University of Nebraska Press, 1999, p. 6.
43. Quoted in Symonds, *Gettysburg*, p. 21.
44. Quoted in Foote and the Editors of Time-Life, *The Civil War*, p. 44.
45. Quoted in Symonds, *Gettysburg*, p. 25.
46. Ibid.

CHAPTER 4

47. Quoted in John Pimlott, ed., *The Hutchison Atlas of Battle Plans: Before and After*. Oxford, UK: Helicon Publishing, 1998, p. 196.
48. Ibid., pp. 196-97.
49. Quoted in John M. Taylor, *Duty Faithfully Performed: Robert E. Lee and His Critics*. Dulles, VA: Brassey's, 2000, p. 142.

50. Quoted in Harry W. Pfanz, *Gettysburg—The First Day*. Chapel Hill, NC: University of North Carolina Press, 2001, p. 51.

51. Ibid.

52. Quoted in Foote and the Editors of Time-Life, *The Civil War*, p. 57.

53. Quoted in Grimsley and Simpson, *Gettysburg*, p. 14.

54. Quoted in Edward J. Stackpole and Wilbur S. Nye, *The Battle of Gettysburg: A Guided Tour*. Revised by Bradley M. Gottfried. Mechanicsburg, PA: Stackpole Books, 1998, p. 49.

55. Quoted in Pfanz, *Gettysburg—The First Day*, p. 77.

56. Quoted in Grimsley and Simpson, *Gettysburg*, p. 20.

57. Ibid.

58. Quoted in Foote and the Editors of Time-Life, *The Civil War*, p. 68.

59. Ibid., p. 70.

60. Quoted in Grimsley and Simpson, *Gettysburg*, p. 20.

61. Quoted in Rod Gragg, *Covered with Glory: The 26th North Carolina Infantry at Gettysburg*. New York: HarperCollins Publishers, 2000, p. 132.

62. Ibid., p. 135.

63. Quoted in Symonds, *Gettysburg*, p. 37.

64. Quoted in Taylor, *Duty Faithfully Performed*, p. 143.

CHAPTER 5

65. Quoted in Stackpole and Nye, *The Battle of Gettysburg*, p. 65.

66. Quoted in Symonds, *Gettysburg*, p. 40.

67. Quoted in Harry W. Pfanz, *Gettysburg: The Second Day*. Chapel Hill, NC: University of North Carolina Press, 1987, p. 26.

68. Quoted in Taylor, *Duty Faithfully Performed*, p. 145.

69. Quoted in Military History Online, 2000, *www.militaryhistoryonline.com/gettysburg/day2/getty21/asp*.

70. Quoted in Stackpole and Nye, *The Battle of Gettysburg*, p. 75.

71. Quoted in Pfanz, *Gettysburg: The Second Day*, p. 201.

72. Ibid., p. 205.

73. Ibid., p. 206.

74. Ibid., p. 173.

75. Quoted in *www.militaryhistoryonline.com/gettysburg/day2/getty22/asp*.

76. Quoted in Stackpole and Nye, *The Battle of Gettysburg*, p. 78.

77. Joshua Lawrence Chamberlain, *Blood & Fire at Gettysburg*. Gettysburg, PA: Stan Clark Military Books, 1994, pp. 22-23.

78. Ibid., p. 23.

79. Quoted in Foote and the Editors of Time-Life, *The Civil War*, p. 107.

80. Chamberlain, *Blood & Fire at Gettysburg*, p. 59.

CHAPTER 6

81. Quoted in Grimsley and Simpson, *Gettysburg*, p. 81.

82. Quoted in Pfanz, *Gettysburg: The Second Day*, p. 193.

83. Quoted in Grimsley and Simpson, *Gettysburg*, p. 83.

84. Quoted in Pfanz, *Gettysburg: The Second Day*, p. 200.

85. Quoted in Foote and the Editors of Time-Life, *The Civil War*, p. 112.

86. Ibid., p. 109.

87. Ibid., p. 112.

88. Ibid., p. 113.

89. Quoted in Grimsley and Simpson, *Gettysburg*, p. 104.

90. Taylor, *Duty Faithfully Performed*, p. 149.

91. Quoted in ibid.

92. Quoted in Emory M. Thomas, *Bold Dragoon: The Life of J. E. B. Stuart*. Norman, OK: University of Oklahoma Press, 1999, p. 246.

CHAPTER 7

93. Quoted in Symonds, *Gettysburg*, p. 62.

94. Quoted in Earl J. Hess, *Pickett's Charge—The Last Attack at Gettysburg*. Chapel Hill, NC: University of North Carolina Press, 2001, p. 33.

95. Quoted in Jeffry D. Wert, *Gettysburg: Day Three*. New York: Simon & Schuster, 2001, p. 30.

96. Ibid.

97. Quoted in Harry W. Pfanz, *Gettysburg—Culp's Hill and Cemetery Hill*. Chapel Hill, NC: University of North Carolina Press, 1993, p. 291.

98. Ibid., p. 300.

99. Ibid., p. 327.

100. Quoted in Taylor, *Duty Faithfully Performed*, p. 150.

101. Ibid.

102. Quoted in Hess, *Pickett's Charge*, p. 149.

103. Ibid., p. 162.

104. Quoted in Fred E. Vandiver, "The Battle of Gettysburg," in *The Oxford Companion to American Military History*. Edited by John Whiteclay Chambers II. New York: Oxford University Press, 1999, p. 298.

105. Quoted in Hess, *Pickett's Charge*, p. 261.

106. Quoted in Symonds, *Gettysburg*, p. 73.

107. Quoted in Stackpole and Nye, *The Battle of Gettysburg*, p. 104.

108. Ibid., p. 108.

109. Quoted in Wert, *Gettysburg*, p. 267.

110. Quoted in Roy Morris, Jr., "Cavalry Clash at Gettysburg." *Military History*, April 1998, p. 43.

111. Ibid.

112. Ibid.

113. Quoted in Kinsley, *Custer*, p. 151.

114. Ibid.

115. Ibid.

116. Ibid., pp. 151-52.

117. Quoted in Morris, "Cavalry Clash at Gettysburg." *Military History*, April 1998, p. 44.

CHAPTER 8

118. Quoted in Taylor, *Duty Faithfully Performed*, p. 155.

119. Quoted in Vandiver, "The Battle of Gettysburg," in *The Oxford Companion to American Military History*, p. 298.

120. Quoted in Pratt, *A Short History of the Civil War*, p. 229.

121. Quoted in Symonds, *Gettysburg*, p. 87.

BOOKS

Catton, Bruce, *The Civil War*. The American Heritage Library. New York: American Heritage Press, 1985.

Chamberlain, Joshua Lawrence, *Blood & Fire at Gettysburg*. Gettysburg, PA: Stan Clark Military Books, 1994.

Chambers II, John Whiteclay, ed., *The Oxford Companion to American Military History*. New York: Oxford University Press, 1999.

Clinton, Catherine, *Scholastic Encyclopedia of the Civil War*. New York: Scholastic, 1999.

Colbert, Nancy A., *The Firing on Fort Sumter: A Splintered Nation Goes to War*. Greensboro, NC: Morgan Reynolds, 2001.

Eggenberger, David, *An Encyclopedia of Battles: Accounts of Over 1,560 Battles from 1479 B.C. to the Present*. Mineola, NY: Dover Publications, 1985.

Foote, Shelby, and the Editors of Time-Life, *The Civil War: A Narrative*. Vol. 7, Gettysburg to Draft Riots, 40th Anniversary Edition. Alexandria, VA: Time-Life Books, 1999.

Freeman, Douglas Southall, *Lee's Lieutenants: A Study in Command*. Vol. 1 *Manassas to Malvern Hill*. New York: Charles Scribner's Sons, 1942.

Gragg, Rod, *Covered with Glory: The 26th North Carolina Infantry at Gettysburg*. New York: HarperCollins Publishers, 2000.

Grimsley, Mark, and Brooks D. Simpson, *Gettysburg: A Battlefield Guide*. Lincoln, NE: University of Nebraska Press, 1999.

Henig, Gerald S., and Eric Niderost, *Civil War Firsts: The Legacies of America's Bloodiest Conflict*. Mechanicsburg, PA: Stackpole Books, 2001.

Hess, Earl J., *Pickett's Charge—The Last Attack at Gettysburg*. Chapel Hill, NC: University of North Carolina Press, 2001.

Kinsley, D. A., *Custer: Favor the Bold, A Soldier's Story*. New York: Promontory Press, 1992.

Matloff, Maurice, ed., *American Military History*. Vol. 1, 1775-1902. Conshohocken, PA: Combined Books, 1996.

Neely, Jr., Mark E., *The Abraham Lincoln Encyclopedia*. New York: Da Capo Press, 1982.

Pfanz, Harry W., *Gettysburg—The First Day*. Chapel Hill, NC: University of North Carolina Press, 2001.

———, *Gettysburg—Culp's Hill and Cemetery Hill*. Chapel Hill, NC: University of North Carolina Press, 1993.

———, *Gettysburg—The Second Day*. Chapel Hill, NC: University of North Carolina Press, 1987.

Pimlott, John, ed., *The Hutchison Atlas of Battle Plans: Before and After*. Oxford, UK: Helicon Publishing, 1998.

Pratt, Fletcher, *A Short History of the Civil War: Ordeal by Fire*. Mineola, NY: Dover Publications, 1997.

Stackpole, Edward J., and Wilbur S. Nye, *The Battle of Gettysburg: A Guided Tour*. Revised by Bradley M. Gottfried. Mechanicsburg, PA: Stackpole Books, 1998.

Stewart, Gail B., *Weapons of War: The Civil War*. American War Library. San Diego, CA: Lucent Books, 2000.

Symonds, Craig L., *Gettysburg: A Battlefield Atlas*. Baltimore, MD: Nautical & Aviation Publishing, 1999.

Taylor, John M., *Duty Faithfully Performed: Robert E. Lee and His Critics*. Dulles, VA: Brassey's, 2000.

Thomas, Emory M., *Bold Dragoon: The Life of J. E. B. Stuart*. Norman, OK: University of Oklahoma Press, 1999.

Wert, Jeffry D., *Gettysburg: Day Three*. New York: Simon & Schuster, 2001.

———— *Custer: The Controversial Life of George Armstrong Custer*. New York: Simon & Schuster, 1996.

PERIODICALS

Morris, Jr., Roy, "The Fishhook's Deadly Barb." *Military History*, August 2001, pp. 26-32.

———— "Cavalry Clash at Gettysburg." *Military History*, April 1998, pp. 39-44.

INTERNET SOURCES

Military History Online, 2000.
[www.militaryhistoryonline.com/gettysburg]

Rush's Lancers, "The Sixth Pennsylvania Cavalry at the Battle of Brandy Station, June 9, 1863," 2000.
[www.rushslancers.com/brandy/html]

Ambrose, Stephen E., *Americans at War*. Jackson, MS: University Press of Mississippi, 1997.

Boyer, Paul S., *The Oxford Companion to United States History*. New York: Oxford University Press, 2001.

Bradley, Mark L., *This Astounding Close: The Road to Bennett Place*. Chapel Hill, NC: University of North Carolina Press, 2000.

Catton, Bruce, *The American Heritage New History of the Civil War*. New York: Viking, 1996.

Commager, Henry Steele, ed., *The Civil War Archive: The History of the Civil War in Documents*. Revised and expanded by Erik Bruun. New York: Black Dog & Leventhal Publishers, 2000.

Cowley, Robert, ed., *With My Face to the Enemy: Perspectives on the Civil War*. New York: G. P. Putnam's Sons, 2001.

——— , *What If? The World's Foremost Military Historians Imagine What Might Have Been*. New York: G. P. Putnam's Sons, 1999.

Cowley, Robert, and Geoffrey Parker, eds., *The Reader's Companion to Military History*. New York: Houghton Mifflin, 1996.

Davis, Paul K., *100 Decisive Battles: From Ancient Times to the Present*. New York: Oxford University Press, 1999.

Davis, William C., *Lincoln's Men: How President Lincoln Became Father to an Army and a Nation*. New York: The Free Press, 1999.

Gallagher, Gary W., ed., *The Third Day at Gettysburg and Beyond*. Chapel Hill, NC: University of North Carolina Press, 1994.

Gauch, Patricia Lee, *Thunder at Gettysburg*. New York: Bantam Doubleday Dell, 1994.

Hutton, Paul Andrew, *The Custer Reader*. Lincoln, NE: University of Nebraska Press, 1992.

Kantor, MacKinlay, *Gettysburg*. New York: Random House, 1952.

Katcher, Philip, *American Civil War Artillery 1861-1865: Field and Heavy Artillery*. Oxford, UK: Osprey, 2001.

——— , *The Civil War Source Book*. New York: Facts On File, 1995.

Keegan, John, *A History of Warfare*. New York: Alfred A. Knopf, 1994.

Laffin, John, *Brassey's Dictionary of Battles*. New York: Barnes & Noble, 1995.

Leckie, Robert, *The Wars of America*. Vol. I. New York: HarperCollins, 1992.

Longacre, Edward G., *Custer and His Wolverines: The Michigan Cavalry Brigade, 1861-1865*. Conshohocken, PA: Combined Publishing, 1997.

Morris, Gilbert. *The Gallant Boys of Gettysburg*. Chicago: Moody Press, 1996.

Parker, Geoffrey, ed., *The Cambridge Illustrated History of Warfare: The Triumph of the West*. New York: Cambridge University Press, 1995.

Perrett, Bryan, *The Battle Book: Crucial Conflicts in History from 1469 BC to the Present*. London: Arms and Armour, 1992.

Pride, Mike, and Mark Travis, *My Brave Boys: To War with Colonel Cross and the Fighting Fifth*. Hanover, NH: University Press of New England, 2001.

Urwin, Gregory J. W., *Custer Victorious: The Civil War Battles of General George Armstrong Custer*. East Brunswick, NJ: Associated University Presses, 1983.

Utley, Robert M., *Cavalier in Buckskin: George Armstrong Custer and the Western Military Frontier*. The Oklahoma Western Biographies, Richard W. Etulain, General Editor. Norman, OK: University of Oklahoma Press, 1988.

Weighley, Russell F., *A Great Civil War: A Military and Political History, 1861-1865*. Bloomington, IN: Indiana University Press, 2000.

Young, Peter, *A Dictionary of Battles (1816-1976)*. New York: Mayflower Books, 1977.

PERIODICALS

O'Beirne, Kevin, "Into the Wheatfield: The Irish Brigade at Gettysburg." *Military Heritage*, October 1999, pp. 40-49, 94.

page:

2:    © Bettmann/Corbis
6:    © Corbis
8:    Hulton Archive by Getty Images
11:   Hulton Archive by Getty Images
13:   Hulton Archive by Getty Images
18:   National Portrait Gallery,
      Smithsonian
21:   © Corbis
23:   Hulton Archive by Getty Images
32:   © Bettmann/Corbis
34:   © Corbis
39:   Hulton Archive by Getty Images
43:   Medford Historical Society
      Collection/Corbis
48:   Hulton Archive by Getty Images
52:   National Archives

54:   reprinted from "The Battle of
      Gettysburg" Harry Pfanz, map
      by George Skoch
62:   painting by Don Troiani,
      www.historicalartprints.com
66:   National Archives
71:   Medford Historical Society
      Collection
77:   © Corbis
83:   National Archive
86:   Painting by Don Troiani,
      www.historicalartprints.com
96:   © Corbis
98:   © Corbis
102: © Bettmann/Corbis

Cover: © Bettmann/Corbis
Frontis: © Bettmann/Corbis

EARLE RICE JR. is a former senior design engineer and technical writer in the aerospace industry. After serving nine years with the U.S. Marine Corps, he attended San Jose City College and Foothill College on the San Francisco Peninsula. He has devoted full time to his writing since 1993 and has written more than 30 books for young adults. Earle is a member of the Society of Children's Book Writers and Illustrators (SCBWI); the League of World War I Aviation Historians and its UK-based sister organization, Cross & Cockade International; the United States Naval Institute; and the Air Force Association.